High Noon on

To the memory of my mother.

High Noon on High Street

Stephen Coyle

Clydeside Press

Printed by Clydeside Press, 37 High Street, Glasgow G1 1LX

Contents

Acknowledgements

I could not have completed this book had it not been for the encouragement of people in Glasgow and Ireland whose participation added colour, substance and human interest to the documents, books, journals and newspapers which form the story and context of the prison rescue attempt. They shared my desire to bring the story to a wider audience and shed some light on a neglected aspect of the history of Glasgow and overlapping histories of Scotland and Ireland.

There are two people without whom this book would never have been written. I am immensely grateful to Cathleen Knowles McGuirk for her generosity of spirit in giving me privileged access to the valuable private papers of her late father Commandant Éamonn Mooney of the Scottish Brigade. I owe a huge debt of gratitude to my friend Dr. Máirtín Ó Catháin for supplying me with copies of witness statements held by the Bureau of Military History in Cathal Brugha Barracks in Dublin. I also benefited from his academic expertise which enabled me to make several improvements to the content. I thank Elaine McDougall for her patience in correcting my spelling and grammar whilst reading the drafts.

I wish to express my gratitude to the staff of the following libraries and archives, without which meaningful historical research could not have been achieved, and for permission to reproduce illustrations and copyright material. The Glasgow Room of the Mitchell Library, Glasgow Caledonian University Research Collections, Heatherbank Museum of Social Work, Sligo County Library, National Archives of Scotland and Public Records Office in Kew.

I wish to thank the Scottish *Daily Record* for kindly giving me permission to include the montage on the front cover.

I am grateful to Hugh MacDonald for allowing me to reproduce the medal belonging to him on the front cover. It was produced by the Irish government to mark the 50th Anniversary of the signing of the Anglo-Irish Treaty, and was issued to surviving veterans of the War of Independence, that is, the men and women who already held the 1919-1921 Service Medals. This would have included the veterans who served in the ranks of the Scottish Brigade of the IRA.

6

The commemorative medal is gilt coloured bronze in the same general design as the 1919-1921 medal, but slightly smaller in size. It is officially known as 'The Truce Commemorative Medal 1971'. The obverse of the medal shows a figure in typical Volunteer dress of the period. Surrounding the figure are the arms of the four provinces of Ireland. The word Éire is spread across the field, whilst the words 'COGAD NA SAOIRSE' ('the fight for freedom') are below the figure. The reverse of the medal is plain with a spray of palm around the left edge. The ribbon has green edges, orange body and black centre strip and hangs from a bronze brooch bearing an interlaced Celtic design.

I have made every reasonable effort to contact the copyright holders of material reproduced in this book. If any involuntary infringement of copyright has occurred, sincere apologies are offered and the owners of such copyright are requested to contact me.

I am indebted to the following individuals who helped in a variety of ways: Jim Friel, Gearoid Mooney, Michael Farry, Seán Feeney, John Cooney, Dr. Tim McGuinness, Colm MacRory, Patrick McAleer and Gerry MacGregor.

All errors and omissions are, of course, entirely my own.

Preface

This book is a labour of love and has taken over a decade to bring to fruition. It is the story of a daring attempt by members of the Irish Republican Army to rescue one of their comrades from a prison van in broad daylight in the centre of Glasgow on the 4th of May 1921. In the mêlée they killed a police inspector and wounded a detective sergeant but failed to release the prisoner from the van.

At the time the episode caused a sensation throughout Scotland and a great deal of indignation was vented in the Scottish press, who referred to it as the 'Glasgow Outrage' and the 'Glasgow Atrocity'. The official name given to the incident was the 'Glasgow Prison Van Case'. The ambush is embedded in Glasgow Irish folklore and immortalised in the street ballad known as the 'The Smashing of the Van'.

The prison van incident has been mentioned in numerous books and newspaper articles, mostly Glasgow crime stories, where the dramatic events of that fateful day are retold in just as sensational a manner as when it was first reported.[1] What most of these accounts have in common is that they treat the ambush as a heinous crime and the participants as ruthless criminals. What is lacking is a failure to address the political context of the ambush, which was the Irish War of Independence that reached its high-water mark in 1921.

This book is a sympathetic account of the ambush, which seeks to explain both the political context and the strong motivation of the young Irish men involved in the rescue bid, who viewed themselves as dedicated and sincere patriots. It recognises that the death of Inspector Robert Johnston of the Glasgow Police was both unintentional and tragic.

The book also aims to set the record straight by giving an account of the ambush from the perspective of the Irish Republicans who planned and executed it. It will show that the Irish community in Scotland was intensely loyal to the All-Ireland Republic that was established with a popular mandate from the people in January 1919. It will reveal the extent to which many of the first, second and third generation Irish living in Scotland were involved in a clandestine network which managed to channel impressive amounts of money, arms, explosives and volunteers across the Irish Sea to sustain the All-Ireland Republic. The book will also convey the sense of paranoia that was felt on the part of the political establishment in London who were fearful of the possibility of a revolutionary situation emerging on Clydeside, involving the combined forces of militant labour, Scottish nationalism and Irish Republicanism.

Notes

1. The rescue attempt is retold in the following books and newspaper articles: Burrowes, John, 'The Glasgow Shinners', *Irish: The Remarkable Saga of a Nation and a City*, Mainstream Publishing, Edinburgh, 2003; Burrowes, John, 'The Glasgow Outrage', *Great Glasgow Stories*, Mainstream Publishing, Edinburgh, 1998; Foreman, Carol, 'Police Inspector Shot Dead in High Street', *Glasgow Curiosities,* John Donald Publishers Ltd, Edinburgh, 1998; Grant, Douglas, *The Thin Blue Line: The Story of the Glasgow Police*, John Long, London, 1973; O'Hagan, Andrew, *The Missing*, Picador, 1995; Skelton, Douglas, 'Ambush', *Blood On the Thistle*, Mainstream Publishing, Glasgow, 1992; 'Battle of Rottenrow', *Daily Record*, 24 April 2006, 'High Noon in High Street', *Evening Times*, 9 December 1989; 'Crimes that Shocked Scotland', *Evening Times*, 14 October 1997.

Chapter 1

Historical Background

To understand the political context in which the prison van was ambushed, it is necessary to turn to events in Ireland in the lead-up to and during the Anglo-Irish War (also known as the War of Independence and the Tan War) and the organised response of Irish Republicans in Scotland to those developments.

At the start of the twentieth century the island of Ireland was still one country of 32 counties, although not a free and independent nation. It had been wholly integrated into the United Kingdom despite a long history of resistance to English rule. Since the dissolution in 1800 of the brief home-ruled parliament in Dublin, accompanied by massive bribes and corruption, there had always been Irish MPs sitting in the House of Commons, and all Ireland was governed directly from Westminster.

However, the spirit of rebellion, existing ever since the Anglo-Norman invasion in 1169, was kept alive throughout the nineteenth century so that by 1912 successive British governments had come to realise that some restoration of home rule was necessary in the hope of thwarting complete independence.

By 1900 the Irish Republican Brotherhood (IRB) was well in decline and what had once been a fighting force was now a group of old men reminiscing about military defeats. The nadir of the IRB's fortunes came in 1912 and this coincided with the introduction of the third Home Rule Bill, when the organisation only had a paying membership of 1,660 in Ireland and 200 in Scotland.

In January 1913 the Unionists in Ulster formed the Ulster Volunteer Force, the purpose of which was to provide an effective military opposition to Home Rule. Eoin MacNeill recommended the formation of a similar force and at a meeting attended by over 30,000 people in the Rotunda in Dublin in November 1913; four thousand names were handed in to enrol in the National Volunteer Force, which pledged itself to defend Home Rule from the UVF threat.

10

Ten days later on December 4th, 1913 a Government proclamation forbade the importation of arms or ammunition into Ireland. The Government had watched Carson's drilling and arming for eleven months without saying a word. When Nationalist Ireland followed suit, they acted at once.

Although strongly influenced by John Redmond and the constitutional nationalists of the Irish Parliamentary Party, the new body was extensively infiltrated by the IRB. By October 1914, there were over 2,000 volunteers in Scotland. When the First World War broke out, Redmond pledged the volunteers to the British war effort, precipitating a split in the organisation. The rupture in Ireland was replicated in Scotland with the bulk going over to the Redmond camp. The remaining Irish Volunteers had two companies in Glasgow by 1915. They drilled in a hall at 34 Ann Street in the Gallowgate.

Arthur Griffith founded Sinn Féin in 1905 and members of the IRB formed a branch in Glasgow within the year. Its first headquarters was a hall at 26 High Street. The Glasgow members tended to be more left wing than the organisation in Ireland and three prominent members, Charles Carrigan, Dan Branniff and Tom White, were members of the Catholic Socialist Society. Up until after the Rising itself, Sinn Féin made little headway in Scotland, the bulk of the Irish placing their hopes in the Home Rule Bills getting passed.

In 1908 a slua (troop) of the Republican scouting organisation Na Fianna Éireann named after the boy patriot and Presbyterian Willie Nelson who was hanged for his part in the 1798 rising, was formed in Glasgow and drilled in a hall in High Street. Another slua was established in Govan. These developments took place at a time when the only other branches of the Fianna were in Dublin, Belfast and Waterford.

In the months immediately preceding the Easter Rising, the Republicans in Scotland were industriously preparing for the momentous events that lay ahead and there was an upsurge in explosive gathering raids and smuggling operations on the part of the IRB. The Fianna transported large amounts of explosives, detonators, fuse wire and other materials useful in bomb making. After storage in "safe" houses in Scotland, young Fianna boys would take the material to Belfast via Ardrossan. Some of the smuggled

11

explosives would be distributed amongst sympathisers in Belfast, but the bulk would be taken to Dublin.

By the start of 1916 the IRB had 10 circles in Scotland based in Lanarkshire, Renfrewshire and Ayrshire. In January of that year the IRB Military Council in Dublin set a date for the Rising.[1] The leadership in Scotland was immediately informed and those who possessed specialist knowledge of explosives left for Ireland. Two such batches of Volunteers (for almost all IRB men were members) departed from Glasgow in January and others followed them in piecemeal fashion in the lead up to Easter.[2] Military conscription was introduced in January so whenever a Volunteer was notified to report for service in the Glasgow contingent of the British Army he would slip across to Ireland beforehand. In Dublin, where almost all the Volunteers from Scotland went, they organised themselves as the Scottish Division of the Kimmage Garrison. They numbered between fifty and sixty and spent the time making and preparing weaponry of various types, drilling and keeping fit. The Kimmage Garrison was formed at the end of 1915 and was commanded by and based at the home of George Plunkett in Larkfield House on the south side of Dublin. Patrick Pearse called the garrison "Ireland's first standing army since the days of Patrick Sarsfield."[3] It comprised mostly of Volunteers from Scotland and England and they were later deployed in garrisons on the perimeter of the GPO and elsewhere. It was a Glasgow steeplejack Paddy Moran that Pearse nominated to hoist the flag of the Irish Republic on the flagpole of the GPO.[4]

Several men who 'had come from a land beyond the sea' never returned. Charles Carrigan, a member of the IRB from Denny in Stirlingshire was killed during the second evacuation of the GPO and the Edinburgh born Commander-in-Chief of the Republican forces, James Connolly, was executed for his part in leading the Rising. Margaret Skinnider from Coatbridge who was a member of both Cumann na mBan and the Irish Citizen Army was severely wounded in the fighting. She had been very active in smuggling explosives and attached herself to the ICA garrison in the College of Surgeons as they, unlike the Volunteers, allowed women to engage in actual combat.

| James Connolly | Charles Carrigan | Margaret Skinnider |

Following the Republican defeat, cattle boats to Britain conveyed the captured members of the Scottish Division, together with nearly two thousand other internees and other deportees, many of whom had been totally uninvolved in the Rising. After a period of dispersal across the British prison system, most were eventually confined together in the Frongoch Internment Camp in Wales which became in effect the 'University' of Irish Republicanism.

The Easter Rising was to become the catalyst for the greatest crisis in Ireland since the rising of 1798, but this was far from apparent at the time.

The reaction in Dublin and of the wider Irish Diaspora to the Rising was one of widespread condemnation of the insurgents. Several newspapers served the Irish community in Scotland. Charles Diamond, who published various local editions in areas served by large Irish populations, mainly owned these. Diamond writing in the *Glasgow Observer* was forthright in his damning criticism, "The Irish People will not manifest the slightest sympathy or approval of the madly criminal actions of the pro German plotters who resorted to insurrection. The actions of the Dublin revolters...was needless, foolish, wicked and unjustifiable. Irish nationalists will condemn it as unpatriotic folly; rash, blind, headlong, stupid and wrong."[5]

The unequivocal denunciations of the Rising on all sides seemed to indicate that the event would be consigned to a mere footnote in Irish history, and yet within two years 'the Sinn Féin banner became the rallying point for nearly every nationalist group, whether moderate or extremist, peaceful or violent.'[6]

The English authorities assisted the decimation of the Parliamentary Party by the indiscriminate character of the arrests and deportations after the Rising. Whether they herded them as convicted prisoners in gaols, or as unconvicted prisoners in concentration camps, the result was the same. The inspiration of a bravely fought battle steeled the prisoners to struggle unflinchingly against every attempt to treat them with humiliation. Struggle begot solidarity, which found expression in organisation. The gaols and concentration camps were so many training schools for a new movement: and when the untried prisoners were released, at Christmas 1916, they dispersed to their homes in every part of Ireland and to lands beyond the sea, including Scotland, convinced Republicans eager to be at work building local organisations in preparation for a new rising.

Six months later, in compliance with American opinion, which it was now imperative to placate, the convicted prisoners were released also to be received with demonstrations of great enthusiasm by the people, who now realised that it was the Men of Easter Week and not their Parliamentarian enemies who had truly represented the will and interest of Ireland.

The men first released at once set to work to build an organisation. A Prisoners' Aid Society was a good beginning: the Gaelic League branches were good rallying centres for a start. The Volunteers began to re-form, and to parade in uniform – but armed only with hurleys and sticks – in spite of proclamations and arrests. The convicted prisoners were in great demand, after their release, as speakers at meetings and demonstrations. Soon the English authorities were at work arresting speakers for "creating disaffection" and Volunteers for "illegal drilling" under the repressive Defence of the Realm Act.

The new mood of the nation showed itself in the attitude of the arrested men. They refused to recognise the jurisdiction of the court; and in gaol demanded the treatment of political prisoners, answering refusal with hunger strike. The death of one of the prisoners, Thomas Ashe (distinguished in Easter Week), evoked great indignation and brought an immense gathering to his funeral, which was made a military one. Three volleys were fired over the grave. Michael Collins (now leader of the revived and powerful IRB) said, "Those volleys we have just heard are the only speech it is fitting to make above the grave of a dead Fenian".[7]

14

Bowing to the inevitable, the authorities conceded political status to the prisoners. Still the struggle went on. Sinn Féin was reorganised, but with an entirely new constitution and programme. De Valera, the only surviving Commandant of Easter Week, was elected as its President at the Annual Convention in October 1917, with Arthur Griffith accepting the position of Vice-President. New ground was broken by (a) the decision to maintain the Volunteers; (b) the tacit adoption of a Republican standpoint, and (c) the tacit decision that the Volunteers would resist forcibly any attempt to impose conscription. The hegemony of the new Sinn Féin Executive, as virtually the Government of the Irish Nation, was recognised by the Gaelic League, and many other Irish National organisations.

In the middle of 1918 Lloyd George attempted to impose conscription in Ireland. Beaten in the House of Commons on this issue, the Parliamentary Party decided to withdraw from Westminster.

A conference met at the Mansion House, Dublin, attended by representatives of Sinn Féin, Labour, the Nationalist Party, and the All for Ireland Party, and the delegates adopted unanimously a pledge to join in common action against conscription. The hierarchy, and the College of Maynooth, concurred with the decision.

Thus Lloyd George's design (which was to smash up the reviving Volunteers) did more than fail: it united all sections of Nationalist Ireland in resistance.

Lloyd George fell back on the trick of "discovering" a German plot. All the leaders of Sinn Féin who could be picked up were hustled into gaol on a charge of "associating with the enemy". The warrant for the arrest of Michael Collins could not be served. He had begun his life on the run which was to last till the Truce of 1921.

Labour showed its determination and power by calling a one-day General Strike, which was enthusiastically observed everywhere in Ireland outside the Unionist areas of the North. Collins set to work to build a General Staff which would direct the resistance of the Volunteers to every attempt to conscript or disarm them. Whatever the reason, the attempt to impose conscription was delayed, on various pretexts, until the ending of the war made it unnecessary.

A number of by-elections since Easter Week might have been taken as a warning of what was coming; they were, however, treated as "wartime" elections which "prove nothing". Count Plunkett whose son was one of the executed 1916 leaders was elected for North Roscommon in a three-cornered contest. Joe McGuinness (then in gaol) was elected for Longford. A much sharper test was the election for Clare to fill the vacancy created by the death of W. E. Redmond. De Valera (sentenced for life) was elected by a two-to-one majority. W.T. Cosgrave (an Easter Week man, then in gaol) was elected for Kilkenny.

Twenty-five seats were surrendered to the Republicans without a struggle. The rest went down like corn before the sickle.

In the general election of December 1918, Sinn Féin consigned the constitutional nationalists of the Irish Parliamentary Party to history, winning 73 out of 105 seats. It moved quickly to implement its policies, clearly outlined in its election manifesto, "to make use of any and every available means to render impotent the power of England to rule Ireland in subjection by military power or otherwise". The manifesto went on to declare that, "Sinn Féin stands less for a political party than for the nation".[8]

The newly elected Republicans met in Dublin and constituted themselves Dáil Éireann - the Governing Body of "the Republic established in Easter Week".

The completeness of the Republican victory at the polls was greater even than it seemed. Every endeavour had been made by the English authorities to prevent it. Election meetings were prohibited, election agents and speakers were arrested, election addresses were censored or suppressed and election literature was confiscated. Warnings against electing Sinn Féin candidates were posted and scattered from aeroplanes. Of the 73 Republicans elected, 36 were in gaol and a score were either "on the run" or in the USA, evading arrest. In these circumstances, to poll two-thirds of all the voters in Ireland for Republican candidates was doubly decisive.

Those of the elected who were at liberty decided to invoke an Irish National Assembly. Everyone elected in Ireland in 1918 was invited regardless of Party. Only Republicans responded, and the twenty-

16

seven of them who were available met in the Mansion House, Dublin, on January 21, 1919, and constituted themselves Dáil Éireann (the Assembly of Ireland). A declaration was adopted affirming that Ireland is "a sovereign and independent nation"; that a Republic (Saorstat Éireann) had been established in Easter Week, 1916, of which the Dáil constituted itself the heir and continuation. The Dáil adopted a "Democratic Programme", which showed profoundly the influence of Connolly and Pearse.[9]

An Acting President was appointed (Cathal Brugha) who had the power to appoint ministers – it being understood that the post of President was left open for Éamon de Valera, then in gaol and whose escape was being contrived at that moment by Michael Collins. On March 5 all prisoners and internees were released.

The situation then was that there were two "Government" authorities in Ireland: one Dáil Éireann, backed by the moral authority of a majority of the people, the other that of the English Authorities, operating from Dublin Castle, who possessed the physical force (police, constabulary, army and navy) to impose their decrees. The struggle that developed was therefore, in essence, an attempt by the English authorities, through their armed forces, to coerce the Irish people into withdrawing the moral authority they had given to Dáil Éireann. Subsequent electoral tests marked the result of their efforts.

At a general election in May 1921 there were elected in the Twenty Six Counties 124 Republicans and 4 Unionists. In the Six Counties in this same election, there were elected 6 Republicans, 6 Nationalists and 40 Unionists. This gave an All-Ireland total of 130 Republicans, 6 Nationalists and 44 Unionists.

Tried by the electoral test, the Irish people gave their choice to the Republic persistently and refused it to the English authorities. It was all the more emphatic because, from the middle of 1919 onwards to July 1921, a ferocious war between the forces of the Crown and those of the Republic was to be fought.

The first phase of this war was an attempt by the British to prevent the Dáil from establishing any machinery of Government. The Dáil itself and all its subsidiaries – including a system of arbitration courts it was able to establish in nearly every county in Ireland – were proclaimed "illegal assemblies". The Loan, called for by the Dáil to raise money for the Republican Government and for the campaign for international recognition, was treated as "seditious". Newspapers that published advertisements of the Loan were suppressed, it was an offence to possess or distribute any literature therewith and every endeavour was made to locate the places and names in which the much-oversubscribed loan was banked. Virtually anybody of prominence in the Republican Movement in this period was either on the run or in prison.

Military operations on the Republican side grew out of this constant harrying and pursuit of Republicans. To achieve their end, the English authorities needed an elaborate apparatus of spies, informers, and "intelligence officers". The backbone of this force was supplied by the Royal Irish Constabulary (RIC), whose officers in the rural areas knew everybody and everything that was going on.

To meet, check, and, finally, to defeat this force was the work undertaken by Michael Collins as Director of Intelligence, operating with a force of specially-selected Volunteers as a striking arm, and a network of counter insurgency agents including police spies, or moles, working within the crown's police forces and intelligence services. The execution of key men in the English espionage service aroused intense fury among reactionary English politicians, and their press. It was justified by Collins on the ground that, while the English could replace their soldiers almost interminably, these key men, with their exceptional knowledge, and their ability to identify particular individuals, could not be replaced. In the end Collins succeeded in paralysing the whole English intelligence service in Ireland.

Concurrently with the war of the contending Intelligence Services, the Volunteers developed a series of raids for arms on isolated police-posts, stores, etc., out of which developed a succession of fiercely-fought battles. In this struggle it soon became apparent that the Volunteers – who, from early in 1919 came to be known as the "Army of the Irish Republic", or popularly, the IRA – had the support of the people, man, woman and child. The IRA when hard pressed could rely upon assistance; the RIC and the British military could always expect obstruction. This passive, social pressure produced the result of wholesale resignations from the RIC and this in turn produced a corresponding diminution in the effectiveness of the Crown forces. Troops from England and Scotland, ignorant of the country and totally unacquainted with the people, were no substitute

18

for men who knew every path and track, as well as every individual for twenty miles around. As their sense of impotence grew, the troops degenerated into an undisciplined *banditti* of alien invaders, bent perpetually upon looting and reprisals.[10]

This led in January 1920 to the imposition of a Curfew Order in the towns and the official adoption of a policy of terrorism, operated from March 1920, by the "Black and Tans" and Auxiliaries.

Those were both officially offshoots of the RIC. The first was a special grade of temporary constables, mostly recruited in England, and chosen for preference from the "tough" class. A criminal record was a recommendation. Men imprisoned for crimes of violence had their sentences remitted if they volunteered for service in the "specials".

The Auxiliaries were "Cadets" recruited from ex-officers in the Army, Navy and Air Force. They operated as a separate force of "shock troops". Individually, they ranked as the equal of senior-sergeants in the RIC. Their pay, rations and allowances were double those of the specials – who came to be called "Black and Tans" because of the haphazard mixture of English khaki and RIC black in their uniforms and equipment.

The political significance of the institution of this Black and Tan force – which term came to include, in practice, the Auxiliaries also, and which, it will be noted, had exactly the same social composition as that of the SA and the SS force of Nazi terrorism, and that of Mussolini's *fascisti* – was that, for diplomatic reasons, Lloyd George and his counter-revolutionary backers found it imperative to pretend that nothing was called for in Ireland beyond "police measures". To have agreed with the demand of the military commanders to proclaim Martial Law would have been an admission that Ireland was in general revolt; and that, therefore, the real position of the English authorities was that of an enemy invader in hostile occupation. The Black and Tans were, deliberately, a "fascist" device – which Mussolini, Hitler and others copied – to conceal the fact that, morally, the English invaders were back where they had been in 1169.[11]

The struggle that developed shocked the English people profoundly and revolted the whole world. Murder, arson, torture of prisoners, rape and the systematic beating-up and looting of whole areas developed into a routine of monotonous horror. The IRA fought back with increasing resolution, and in the struggle developed into a force which became able to meet, and defeat, parties of Black and Tans and Auxiliaries on equal terms. The primary IRA tactic was that of the ambush; to which the "Tans" replied by beating-up, looting and destroying the habitations in the area where the ambush occurred. This, of course, drove more recruits to the IRA, and so the struggle developed. The work done by Liam Mellows (of whom we will hear more later), as Director of Purchases, in supplying the IRA with arms-purchased abroad and smuggled into Ireland was an invaluable contribution to the Republican war-effort.

As the RIC dwindled, it retreated from the outlying districts. In these areas, Republican Courts were established whose decisions were accepted by the people. Order was maintained and punishments imposed by the Courts were enforced by the Republican police (IRA volunteers detailed for this duty). These proofs of the impotence of the English authorities and the popular acceptance of the authority of the Dáil, reported in the press of the world, roused the counter-revolutionaries to fury. In those areas, advanced flying squads of Black and Tans in armoured cars resolved to loot, burn, smash, destroy, arrest and kill. If they were resisted – or, more usually, ambushed on their way back, more flying squads repeated the performance, with similar results.

In the bigger towns the Black and Tans had all retreated to barracks from which they emerged only at the risk of attack and ambush in open day. The gaols were crammed with prisoners arrested for conducting Republican Courts, or simply on suspicion. Then, on July 11 1921, Lloyd George and Éamon de Valera, as a preliminary to negotiations for a Treaty, agreed a truce.

Faced with multiplying political difficulties on every side, Lloyd George in 1920 made a gesture towards settling the Irish Question by introducing the long-deferred amendment of the Home Rule Act (1914). This Government of Ireland Act (1920) represented a compromise which the "Ulster" representatives accepted with reluctance. It conceded a measure of Home Rule to the Twenty-Six Counties (called "Southern Ireland") and imposed another measure of Home Rule on the Six Counties (called "Northern Ireland").

The Act included a provision that the two parliaments might, if they chose, set up an All Ireland Council to which each might concede powers of common concern. In this way they could achieve a reunited Ireland. This was merely eye-wash for Americans, English Labour Party men, and other political innocents, who did not know (as Lloyd George did) that the faction dominant in the Six Counties would never consent to any such reunion, since they had a vested interest in Ireland's unsettlement. Dáil Éireann as such took no notice of the Act. But Sinn Féin resolved to use the elections as a demonstration of national unity. The result was that the only non-Republican candidates elected were the four allotted to Trinity College. No contests took place. No one would accept nomination against a Republican.

As a running commentary upon the Tan War and Lloyd George's manoeuvres with the Government of Ireland Act, Belfast staged a series of pogroms, aimed at driving the Catholics out of the industrial area completely. Their opening (July 21, 1920) coincided with the introduction of the Black and Tan Terror; and they had been preceded by inflammatory propaganda meetings, in which it was suggested that the Catholics were "creeping-in", and "were taking away the jobs of Protestants". The beginning of the post-war unemployment crisis gave point to the oratory; and there is no reason to doubt that what followed was organised, as well as deliberately incited.

A corps similar to the Black and Tans had been recruited as "occasional special Constables" by the Six County Government, members of this corps, recruited from the hooligan element in Belfast, were in the front of the mobs which, carrying Union Jacks, attacked the Catholic quarter, looting and burning down the shops and houses of Catholics. Every Catholic was driven from the shipyards, every Catholic worker from the factories where "Protestants" predominated. Any attempt at self-defence was crushed with stones, bludgeons, and revolver or rifle-fire. Only after four days did the military interfere. Twenty-two civilians were killed, and 188 were severely wounded.

The pogrom extended to Lisburn on August 23-24; forty Catholic houses and shops were destroyed. Then the pogrom was renewed in Belfast, August 28 - September 1st, and similar barbarities were enacted. Apart from scores killed, and hundreds of wounded, 9,000

21

were driven from their employment, 30,000 were rendered destitute, and thousands were rendered homeless into the bargain. Hundreds of fleeing refugees came to Glasgow where they were temporarily put up in Catholic Church halls.

Carson's cynical comment virtually admitted Orange-Tory complicity in the pogrom. He said that Catholics "had only to take an oath of allegiance to the King, and pledge their loyalty to the Empire, and the trouble would cease instantly". This meant, if it meant anything, that the Belfast Catholics were to be used as hostages in the war for the new English conquest of Ireland.

The resignation of 148 Irish magistrates as well as mutinies in the police force and of the hundred men of the Connaught Rangers in India, were eloquent, practical comments on the policy pursued in Ireland.

The pogroms broke out again in Belfast in June 1921, after the elections to the Northern Ireland Parliament; in which, as an Ulster-Tory MP said, "too many Sinn Fein votes were cast". The riots were almost entirely the work of Special Constables. A score of Catholics were killed, and another 150 families were rendered homeless.

These atrocities and the steadfast solidarity in the face of every barbarity of the Nationalist population of Ireland had a profound effect upon democratic opinion in England as well as throughout the world.

The Irish community in Scotland's active participation in their ancestral land's revolutionary movements was a deep-rooted tradition. John Denver claimed that several hundred Irishmen armed and prepared themselves to take part in the Young Ireland rebellion in 1848.[12] Later in the century many Irish immigrants who resided in the many "Little Irelands" responded positively to the uncompromising Republican physical force message of the Fenian Movement.[13] The important contribution made by the Irish overseas to the struggle for Irish freedom between the suppression of the Easter Rising of 1916 and the signing of the Anglo-Irish Treaty in 1921 has long been recognised. In particular, the United States played a central role in giving both financial and moral support to the Republican forces.

Several writers have highlighted the significant part played by Republican supporters in Scotland in helping to force Britain to the negotiating table. James Handley, the author of the seminal work, *The Irish in Modern Scotland* recognises the crucial role assigned to Scotland. "A certain amount of gun-running was carried out before 1916 and a considerable number of men and women volunteers went to Dublin for the Easter Rising", Handley wrote, "But it was not until guerrilla fighting broke out in Ireland that sympathisers in Scotland had the opportunity of rendering effective service. That service in money and materials was given so generously that the contribution of Scotland to the Sinn Fein campaign far exceeded that of any other country, including Ireland, and was, in the opinion of Mr de Valera, the chief factor in its success."[14]

Other historians have backed up Handley's judgement. Tom Gallagher has argued that the Irish on Clydeside were allocated by the Republican leadership "a different and more crucial role: they were to provide money and military supplies to keep the war effort going back home and safe houses for IRA men on the run from British or Irish gaols".[15] Patterson notes that this was hardly surprising as there was a very large Irish immigrant population in Scotland - proportionately higher than England, many of whom had only recently arrived.[16] Indeed the 1921 Census showed that there were 65,688 people of Irish birth in Glasgow. In contrast to Handley, Gallagher and Ó Catháin, Patterson is keen to stress the marginality of the IRA in Scotland to the events that occurred in Ireland between 1918 and 1921.

There is a good deal of evidence to indicate the importance of Scotland to the Irish military campaign. There was a Scottish Brigade of the IRA in existence throughout the War of Independence. Michael Collins, the military genius of the IRA was in correspondence with Scotland and furthermore Collins sent over a prominent organiser, Joe Vize, to oversee the Scottish Brigade. Additionally, leading figures such as Liam Mellows and Cathal Brugha spent some time in Scotland between 1919 and 1921.

The main role assigned to the Scottish Brigade by headquarters was to procure much needed military equipment and ammunition and a number of methods were employed to achieve this goal. Every company was required to send a regular quota of revolvers, ammunition, and rifles to headquarters in Glasgow. From quarries,

23

coal pits and shale mines, powder and gelignite were obtained and eight successful raids were carried out on Clyde shipyards engaged in munitions works.[17] Raiding colliery armouries was a favourite means of obtaining explosives and detonators, not least because many Irishmen worked in the mining industry. For instance in December 1920 the IRA broke in to Robroyston Colliery to seize explosives.[18] Another method was to persuade a sympathetic engineer to exaggerate the amount of material needed for a specific contract. He would use the minimum amount necessary and pass over the surplus to the IRA. Raids on premises other than collieries and quarries in search of rifles, explosives and other military equipment were also carried out. British Intelligence reported that arms, ammunition and money had been removed from the Orange Order's hall in the Cowcaddens district of Glasgow. Before leaving the burglars had scrawled the words 'Commandeered for the Irish Republican Army' on the wall.[19] Vize purchased munitions from a variety of sources. One of his major suppliers was Mr J. Corbett of Parkhead, Glasgow, who was a contractor and thus had easy access to gelignite and detonators. He was in a position to employ IRA members as part of his workforce and then train them in the use of explosives. Once the man had mastered the requisite skills, he would return to Ireland to further the Republican cause.[20] One of Vize's favourite ploys was to bribe men in military barracks in Maryhill, Hamilton and Dunfermline. By 1921 the Scottish Brigade comprised 5 battalions and could boast a membership of around 2,500 which included two hundred ex-members of the British Army (see *Appendix 1*).

Cumann na mBan, the female auxiliary organisation of the IRA, was active in Scotland and in 1920 had branches in Broxburn, Govan, Motherwell, Clydebank, Hamilton, Edinburgh, Mossend, Glasgow (B and C companies), Townhead, Uddingston, Parkhead, Cambuslang and Wishaw.[21]

The Irish Citizen Army (ICA) existed in Glasgow despite being largely dormant in Ireland during the Anglo-Irish War. The ICA was set up in 1913 by the Irish Transport and General Workers Union to protect demonstrating workers and pickets from the often-violent attentions of the police during the Dublin lock-out. Members of the Irish Volunteers with socialist republican sympathies assisted in the smuggling of arms to the ICA in Ireland.

24

The decline of constitutional nationalism and the subsequent popularity of the cause of Sinn Féin were replicated in Scotland as shown by the massive growth in Sinn Féin clubs and by the sympathetic response of the Scottish Catholic press under the tutelage of Charles Diamond. Seán O'Sheehan was sent over as a Sinn Féin organiser in 1918. He helped to expand the organisation from one central club in Glasgow in 1917 to seventy five clubs in 1919.[22] The typical activities of a club, which served as a contact centre for immigrants, included holding lectures and debates of Irish interest, commemorating national anniversaries, public meetings and ceilidhs, and the publication and sale of Republican literature.[23]

The high point for Sinn Féin in Scotland came in 1920 with the visit of the Republican supporter Archbishop Daniel Mannix of Australia after he was banned from entry to Ireland, and from speaking in Manchester and Liverpool. The archbishop spoke to large crowds of enthusiastic supporters in Edinburgh, Greenock (where Sinn Féin had 1,000 members), Dalmuir, Kilmarnock, Dumbarton, Cowdenbeath, and Dundee, where Mannix viewed a procession ten miles in length. The Glasgow demonstration was blocked and Mannix spoke to a defiant crowd of 50,000 to 60,000 supporters at Whifflet instead.[24]

Archbishop Daniel Mannix

A number of priests were members of Sinn Féin and some held prominent positions. Church door collections were permitted in many parishes and Requiem Masses were held for Republican martyrs including Terence MacSwiney and Kevin Barry. A report on Sinn Féin activity sent by Secretary for Scotland to John Gilmour MP dated 28/11/1920 records that:

"A Solemn Requiem Mass was celebrated in St Joseph's RC Church, North Woodside Road, in Glasgow for the repose of the soul of Rev. Father Griffin and Kevin Barry murdered by the order of the British Government in order to drive terror into the hearts of the Irish people and kill the soul and spirit of the Irish nation. The Rev. Joseph Reilly was celebrant and the Rev. James McConnell, delivered the panegyric. The Anne Devlin branch of Cumann na mBan, whose members wore dark armlets, arranged the Mass. Two companies of the Irish Volunteers were present, wearing Sinn Féin favours and Volunteer badges. There were present about fifteen hundred persons, a record attendance in this parish for a downright wet morning.

The writer desires to point out that the callous and deliberate murders, the burning of creameries and houses, is exasperating the Irish people of Glasgow to the utmost limit of human endeavour and is straining the bonds of discipline to breaking point. The Irish Volunteers are one of the best disciplined and one of the biggest forces in Scotland and may break out of hand at any moment."[25]

Among the prominent Republicans who visited Scotland during this period were Dan Breen, Lawrence Ginnell, Countess Markievicz, Hanna Sheehy Skeffington, Professor Stockley, Seán Milroy and Margaret Pearse (mother of Patrick).[26]

The Sinn Féin propagandist, P. J. Little, was in Glasgow and established a thriving Republican press after his operation came under increasing pressure in Ireland with the suppression of his *New Ireland* paper in 1919. In Glasgow he produced *Old Ireland* from 1919 to 1921 and involved himself with a host of other papers including *Dark Rosaleen,* which he edited.[27]

This was the period of 'Red Clydeside' and the labour movement was generally supportive of the Irish cause as was demonstrated in 1921 when the Scottish Trades Union Congress at its annual conference in Aberdeen, unanimously passed a resolution calling on the British Government at once to summon a constituent assembly of the Irish people to "get a peaceful settlement, and meanwhile to withdraw the army of occupation".[28] John MacLean the Scottish socialist republican was highly respected among the Irish as a

26

tireless campaigner for Irish freedom amongst the Scottish working class. MacLean argued that, "the withdrawal of Scottish lads from the cold blooded murder of the Irish… is the greatest question confronting Scotland today, for if speedy action is not taken, a horrible tragedy will be enacted, and Scotland will be disgraced forever".[29] In support of these sentiments, he issued a pamphlet, *The Irish Tragedy: Scotland's Disgrace*, which sold 20,000 copies.

The Irish Tragedy:

Scotland's Disgrace..

By

JOHN MACLEAN, M.A.

Price 2d.

Published by

JOHN MACLEAN, 42 AULDHOUSE ROAD,

NEWLANDS, GLASGOW

1920.

:: Proposed ::
IRISH MASSACRE!

SCOTTISH WORKERS, TAKE HEED!

SCOTTISH troops are in Ireland and are in readiness to send to Ireland to murder the Irish race. Why?

Because Ireland wishes the independence our Scottish ancestors fought for under Wallace and Bruce.

Remember Bannockburn and Flodden.

Read again Burns's "Scots Wha Hae."

Remember Knox and Wishart; and the Covenanters who fought the English troops under Claverhouse at Bothwell Brig. What for? Independent religious thinking in Scotland.

Remember that Henry II., in the twelfth century, stole Ireland by force, and Ireland has been ruled by force since. Cromwell and other butchers murdered the Irish before the Orange organisation was formed, purely to prevent Irish Independence.

Remember that Irishmen are as entitled to fight for freedom as we Scots, or as the Swiss under William Tell.

Remember that Irishmen are Celts like the Highlanders and that the English are Germans.

Lloyd George holds Ireland not to protect the Ulstermen, but to prevent America using Ireland in case of war.

Lloyd George said we fought Germany to save Belgium. Sir Henry Wilson now says we fought Germany "to save our own skin."

America wishes trade and empire. Britain stands in the way. America is getting ready. Britain is getting

[P.T.O.

28

MacLean organised 'Hands Off Ireland' demonstrations that attracted crowds of up to 15,000 workers. John Wheatley of the Independent Labour Party, who became the Minister for Health in the first Labour government, joined the campaign and, along with MacLean and Countess Markievicz, addressed the May Day Rally on Glasgow Green in 1919. Irish tricolours were carried openly among a crowd of 100,000 and the 'Soldier's Song' was sung as well as the 'Red Flag'. Later again that year Wheatley spoke at a Hands off Ireland meeting which filled St Andrew's Hall with 5,000 people, leaving another 5,000 outside.[30]

William Gillies

Strong links existed between Sinn Féin and the Scots National League which campaigned for the complete political independence of Scotland and was inspired by the Irish cause. Michael Collins viewed Liam MacGill Iosa (William Gillies), who was a prominent member of both the League and the nationalist volunteer body Fianna na h-Alba, as a "very genuine man".[31] The League's journal *Liberty* contained pro-Irish articles and, ironically, the editor John

29

McArthur, who was a Rangers fan, sold it outside Ibrox Stadium.[32] The League later became one of the groups that combined to found the National Party of Scotland in 1928, the forerunner of today's Scottish National Party.

David Ritchie has recently assessed the attitude of the authorities in Scotland to the Irish Republicans during the Anglo-Irish War. He demonstrated that there were those in senior positions who believed they were in a war situation and that the IRA was capable of deploying a considerable force in the middle of Scotland. He concluded that the authorities had an "almighty fright that ranked alongside the threat of Bolshevik revolution from Clydeside workers".[33]

The following letter from the Chief Constable of Glasgow C.I.D. to Under Secretary of Scotland dated 17 October 1920 is indicative of the anxiety over the perceived IRA threat which was the subject of numerous Cabinet reports and discussions and were raised frequently in the House of Commons.

> *"I have now to report that private information believed to be reliable has been received that a secret meeting of the leaders of the Society (Sinn Fein) was held in the League of the Cross Hall, Patrick St, Greenock, on the night of the 16th inst when 37 Sinn Fein Clubs were represented. It was reported that the strength of the Sinn Fein Volunteers in Glasgow and the West of Scotland was 30,000 and that 20,000 had revolvers, and 2,000 had rifles all of the modern pattern, with unlimited ammunition; that they had plans of Maryhill Barracks and of all the Territorial Drill Halls in Glasgow, Lanarkshire, Renfrewshire and Dunbartonshire.*
>
> *The delegates were instructed to inform their several battalions that an order might be received at any time to mobilise, and to be ready to act either in Ireland or Scotland as might be required."*

In terms of supporting and supplying the IRA, Patterson may have a point when he asserts that "Green Clydeside" posed more of a threat to the unity of the United Kingdom than "Red Clydeside" ever did.[34]

Having provided the political context by summarising the tumultuous political events in early twentieth century Ireland and described the significant response by the Irish in Scotland to those developments, the next chapter will properly begin the story of the dramatic attempt to rescue Frank Carty from a prison van in Glasgow in 1921.

Notes

1. According to Seámus Reader who became the official military representative to Dublin on the Scottish Divisional Board of the IRB, "anti conscription and the intended revolt on the Clyde did influence Countess Markievicz, James Connolly and Seán MacDiarmada. They were determined that at least the Liffy would assert itself." Quoted in 'Scotland and the Easter Rising' by Raymond J. Ross, *Radical Scotland,* June 1986.
2. Máirtín Ó Catháin, *Irish Republicanism in Scotland 1858-1916*, Irish Academic Press, Dublin, 2007, p.238.
3. Michael Maguire, 'From Across the Irish Sea: The Irish in Britain and the Making of 1916' in *1916 - We Remember*, Cumann na Poblachta, London, 1991, p.9.
4. Ann Matthews, 'Vanguard of the Revolution? The Irish Citizen Army 1916' in *The Impact of the 1916 Rising*, Irish Academic Press, Dublin, 2008, p.31.
5. David Ritchie, *Sinn Féin and the Scottish Office 1919-1923*, Ph.D thesis, Edinburgh University, 2008, p.7.
6. Ritchie, ibid, p.8.
7. T.A. Jackson *Ireland Her Own*, Lawrence & Wishart, London, 1976, p.406.
8. Des Dalton, *Sinn Féin 100 Years of Revolution 1905-2005,* Irish Freedom Press, Dublin 2005, p.8.
9. T.A. Jackson, op cit, p.411.
10. The Democratic Programme of the First Dáil provided; for the right of the people of Ireland to the ownership of Ireland and to the unfettered control of Irish destinies; its soil, resources and wealth producing processes; rights of private property to be subordinate to public right and welfare. That the country be ruled by Liberty, Equality, and Justice for all. Every man and woman to give allegiance and service. In return every citizen would have a share of the produce of the nation's labour. Children would be cared for; no child would suffer hunger or cold, lack of clothing or shelter; all to be educated in a free and Gaelic Ireland.
11. T.A. Jackson, op cit, pp.414-415.

12. Iain D. Patterson, The Activities of Irish Republican Physical Force Organisations in Scotland 1919-21, *Scottish Historical Review*, Volume LXXII, No 193, April 1995, p.39.
13. Máirtín Ó Catháin, *Irish Republicanism in Scotland 1858-1916*, Irish Academic Press, 2007, p.238.
14. James E Handley, *The Irish in Modern Scotland*, Cork University Press, 1947, p.297.
15. Tom Gallagher, *Glasgow the Uneasy Peace*, Manchester University Press, 1987, p.91.
16. Patterson, op cit, p.39.
17. Gallagher, op cit, p.91.
18. Patterson, op cit, p41.
19. Patterson, op cit, p41.
20. Patterson, op cit, p41.
21. Patterson, op cit, p53.
22. Máirtín Ó Catháin, *Michael Collins and Scotland*, p.6. To be published in 2009.
23. Roger Casement Sinn Féin Club pamphlet (n.d.)
24. Mairtin O'Cathain, 'A Winnowing Spirit: Sinn Féin in Scotland, 1905-1938', *New Perspectives on The Irish in Scotland*, (ed. Martin J. Mitchell) John Donald, Edinburgh, 2008, p.122.
25. NAS GD383/14/7 Gilmour Correspondence, in Ritchie, p.20.
26. Éamonn Mooney Papers.
27. Máirtín Ó Catháin, *Michael Collins and Scotland*, p.6. To be published in 2009.
28. Angela Tuckett, *The Scottish Trade Union Congress: The First 80 Years 1897-1977*, Mainstream Publishers, Edinburgh, 1986, p.177.
29. Nan Milton, *John MacLean*, Pluto Press, London, 1973, p.238.
30. Ian Wood, *John Wheatley*, Manchester University Press, 1990, p.79.
31. Stephen Coyle, 'Portrait of a Patriot – William Gillies' *Scottish Workers Republic*, Spring 1997; 'Liam MacGill'Iosa: A Friend of the Gael', *Transactions of the Gaelic Society of Inverness*, Professor William Gillies, Volume LVI, Christmas 1992.
32. Richard Finlay, *Independent and Free*, John Donald Publishers, Edinburgh, 1994, p.34.
33. Ritchie, op cit, p.36.
34. Patterson, op cit, p.13.

Brigadier Frank Carty

Chapter 2

The Man in the Van

Frank J. Carty was born in April 1897, the son of John Carty, a farmer of Clooncunny, Ballymote in County Sligo. As a boy, he became attached to the Sinn Féin organisation and was one of the first and most youthful members of the Irish Republican Army in the west of Ireland when he joined in 1914. Six feet tall and of athletic build, he commanded an air of authority. He had scarcely attained manhood when he was appointed Vice-Brigadier of the Sligo Brigade, and in 1921 he was promoted to the rank of Brigadier, 4th Brigade, South Sligo IRA. In the spring of 1920, Carty was captured by the Crown Forces and charged with participation in a daylight raid for arms on the residence of Major Perceval of Templehouse.[1] At the subsequent trial he refused to recognise the jurisdiction of the court, was remanded four times, and eventually returned for trial to Derry Assizes. Whilst awaiting transfer to Derry, he made a dramatic escape from Sligo Jail.

The Rev. William Pilkington, formerly O.C. Sligo Brigade IRA, decided that Carty, his Vice-Brigadier, had already been in prison long enough and embarked on a carefully laid rescue plan, which was executed on June 26, 1920. Sligo was held by strong forces of the enemy. Across the river, about two hundred yards from Cranmore where stood the jail, was the military barracks. There were also two police barracks in the town and their combined RIC and Black and Tan garrisons were at full strength. Breaking into the jail would be the easy part of the job. Getting Carty away safely might be difficult. If the enemy were alerted there would be a gunfight such as Sligo had never seen before. The Town Battalion had, on Pilkington's direction, thrown a ring of barricades and outposts around the jail and covered all the approaches from the barracks. Their orders were to hold off the enemy.

Earlier, Volunteers of the Sligo Town Battalion had put ladders in position near the jail, to be used by the men scaling the jail wall. At zero hour the telephone wires would be cut and, while the assault party went into action to release Frank Carty, the ring of IRA Volunteers would cover the withdrawal.

The armed party of ten, which had come by the road above the cemetery, joined a small body of waiting men and all moved off cautiously through fields above the town. No smoking was permitted. Each man kept close to the man in front of him. They covered ground rapidly, the swish of the dew-wet grass against their boots being the only sound to break the silence of the pitch-black night. Here and there pinpoints of light stabbed the darkness that enveloped the sleepless huddle of the town and warned the column of men that not everybody slept and that, above all, the enemy might be on the alert.

Soon the great hulk of the jail wall loomed high in the darkness and the column halted as its leader held a whispered consultation with a shadowy figure which had materialised as though from nowhere. It was the Brigadier. In a quiet voice which carried down the line, he detailed their duties to the men from the country companies who had volunteered for the dangerous tasks inside the walls. It was essential that the men who went in should not be local men, in case of recognition by warders or others of the prison staff. There had been no lack of volunteers.

"There is a ladder here on the outside," Pilkington told them. "You will climb that and you will find a rope ladder in position in the inside." To two of the party he said, "You will take up positions in the main hall and make sure that the patrol man doesn't ring the alarm bell".

Of the men present, each had a part to play and he knew it to the last detail. Pilkington had seen to that.

The signal was then given for the operation to commence. Massive iron gates, taken from Kilgallon's, a Big House within a quarter mile of the jail, were put in position across the avenue leading to the jail. Twenty men with crowbars, sledge hammers and a pickaxe moved through the darkness to positions outside the wicket gate in the main avenue. Another twenty or more occupied the outpost positions. The telephone wires leading to the jail and to the military and police barracks were cut.

The scaling-ladder squeaked as it was raised and placed firmly in position against the weather-beaten stone of the 32-foot high wall of the jail. Rapidly, thirteen men climbed the ladder which was held securely by two men on the ground. As each man arrived on top of the wall he immediately started down the rope ladder into the jail courtyard.

In the yard they paused for a minute, on the alert for the slightest sound which would indicate that their entry had been detected. Nothing stirred. Not a thing was heard save the soft whistle of the wind around the jail walls.

In his cell Frank Carty waited tensely. Throughout the week Warder O'Connor, who was one of the Brigade contacts inside the wall, had brought messages in to him. In the dimly lit hall sat Chief Warder Hooke, armed but at ease. How could he suspect that desperate men were about to shatter his illusions of the security of Sligo Jail? In his house, separated from the cellblock by an open yard, Governor Reid slept soundly. In the yard beneath the shadow of the wall thirteen men waited breathlessly, each waiting second an hour of suspense.

Thirteen hands gripped gun butts. In mounting tension thirteen men lived an eternity as they waited for a significant sound. At last it came. The sound of the ponderous, assured footsteps of the night patrolman on his rounds. Nearer and nearer came the sound, and now the waiting men could hear the patrolman whistling tunelessly under his breath, his thoughts no doubt, on his meal-break which was due shortly. This was a vital moment. A blunder now and the entire carefully laid rescue plan could be ruined. If the patrolman suspected anything untoward, his whistle would alarm the entire jail and Carty would remain inside, the men in the yard would be trapped, and blood would be spilled in the inevitable gunfight between the IRA and the enemy. Nerves were stretched to breaking point as the patrolman approached. Two figures sneaked silently along in the darkness, so unobtrusively that the waiting men were not sure if they had imagined the movements. Still, not a sound was heard other than that made by the patrolman. Suddenly the plod of his footsteps ceased and the tuneless whistle died in his throat as a rough hand closed firmly over his mouth. Terror and consternation gripped him for he had no doubt that he was in deadly peril. Something was pressed hard into his ribs, and he nodded his head vigorously in acquiescence when a low voice enjoined him to remain silent if he valued his life.

The patrolman was only doing a job. He looked forward to a quiet life and a pension on retirement. He had no wish to be a dead hero for England, and so he remained alive. Trussed up with his own belt on the ground, his back resting against the wall. But he was alive and witness to one of the strangest incidents of his prison career.

The men outside the jail waited, their eyes straining to probe the darkness, their ears attuned to the slightest sound.

Inside the walls the climactic moment of the rescue was at hand. Pilkington, who never raised his voice, never lost his temper, never swore, never permitted a man in his company to swear, was leading the operation personally. Having marked off five of his men, he tapped them on the shoulders as a signal to get going. They skirted the archway with its faint glow of light and vanished into the darkness near the governor's house. Seconds later two men moved into position, their task to maintain communications. Four others crossed the yard in single file, five places between each man. Quietly but purposefully, they headed for the hall where Warder Hooke drowsed in his high chair. Before the warder knew what was happening, Pilkington had poked a pistol into his ribs. Within arm's reach of Hooke was the switch which could set off the brazen clamour of the alarm. But he made no movement towards it. In a flash two men pounced on him and he was bound and gagged and relieved of his keys.

Harry Conroy, later to become one of Michael Collins's intelligence officers, signalled a contact man who doubled across the yard to the governor's house, regardless of the noise he made. When he got inside the house he made straight for the governor's room and saw grey-haired Governor Reid sitting up in bed, hair tousled and his eyes filled with sleepy astonishment following a rude awakening from his slumber. Reid was being menaced by five armed men. Defiant, but with an undertone of fear or uncertainty, he said to them: "Even if I had the keys, I'm blowed if I would give them to you. The governor doesn't keep keys…" The voice tailed off, interrupted by the metallic click of a safety catch being released. "The keys or else…" The keys changed ownership. There was a murmur of voices and a curt order directing two men to secure the governor.

The other three men, with Pilkington in the lead, dashed full pelt across the yard to the cellblock. It was the work of but a moment for

37

one of them to unlock the door to the corridor. In another moment Pilkington had raced down the corridor and turned a key in the lock of Frank Carty's cell. The Vice-Brigadier, dressed for the street, followed him through the corridor and out into the fresh air of the courtyard.

Fourteen men crowded at the foot of the rope ladder in the courtyard. Speed was more essential than ever then, for surely the alarm must be raised any second. None of the men inside the yard could even know for certain whether members of the rescue party had not inadvertently alerted enemy forces on patrol in the town through some action. Even now military and police might be converging on Cranmore.

Brigadier Pilkington decided that escape over the wall by means of the rope ladder would be dangerously slow. Everything had gone well for him. Now he must not risk any of his men being shot or captured as they dangled more or less helplessly from the wall. There was no time to look for the keys to the gate. Pilkington nodded. One of the men, his mouth almost dry with tension, managed to whistle. His shrill note had scarcely ended when the night silence was shattered by the crash of sledge hammers and crowbars on the sturdy wicket gate, as the twenty men on the outside worked with a will to demolish the barrier between Frank Carty and the others of his rescue party and the completion of their mission. The din was deafening. It seemed as though the whole town of Sligo must be awakened and the military in the barracks across the river startled into action. The fourteen men inside the jail checked their weapons.

With a crash like thunder the gate collapsed and Frank Carty and the thirteen others dashed through the gap. As soon as he saw them emerge, Jim Keaveney sped from outpost to outpost, ordering the stand-to parties to dismiss at once. The men from the country companies doubled across the sodden fields and were then driven to their homes in cars that had all lights switched out. The men of the Sligo Town Battalion slipped home and into bed. Frank Carty was whisked out of town. Through all this military activity the jail personnel, the police and the military remained silent and inactive.

It was after one o'clock in the morning and Kilgallon's gates still blocked the avenue to the jail. All was peaceful in Sligo town.

Sometime later the British forces swung into action at long last, in reaction to the rescue. They drove a lorry load of troops at breakneck speed towards the jail and crashed head-on into Kilgallon's gates which still barricaded the entrance. The smash, in which several British soldiers were injured, caused the only casualties in the rescue of Frank Carty.[2]

Carty's sensational escape gave rise to a massive day and night search throughout the county by both police and military, but neither the prisoner nor his rescuers were captured then. The Sligo County Council meeting on July 17 passed a number of resolutions including one of congratulations to Frank Carty on his escape from jail. They also called on all able-bodied men aged between 18 and 40 to join the IRA.[3]

After the rescue Carty commanded a flying column for about five months. During this time he managed to turn up at a meeting of Tubbercurry Rural District Council to which a substantial majority had elected him during his term in prison.

Carty's luck ran out in November of the same year when, in Vessey's House in Moylough, Tubbercurry, he and two others were surrounded by Black and Tans and, following a desperate resistance in which he was wounded in the wrist, he was overpowered and carried off to the maximum security jail in Derry. The walls of Derry Jail, which stood in Bishop Street, were stout and high - about five feet wide and over forty feet high. It opened in 1824 and ceased to be a jail in 1953.

Derry Jail, Bishop Street.

39

Carty was incarcerated there throughout the winter. He was not cut off from events outside, however, for even in Derry Jail the IRA had friends amongst the warders, almost all of whom bought their cigarettes and newspapers in a little tobacconist shop in Bishop Street, outside the main gate. The owner of the shop was an IRA sympathiser and his place became an important unofficial post office; messages left there by IRA Volunteers were passed on and a number of them were slipped to Carty inside the escape-proof fortress.

At this point Chares J McGuinness enters our story. A native of Derry city, his father was a sea captain and he himself was an officer in the North German Lloyd Shipping Line and he spoke German fluently.[4] He was a captain of the collier *Carricklee* on board which Charlie made many trips to smuggle in arms for the IRA; but routine trips between Derry and Glasgow bored the younger McGuinness and he sought adventure with the IRA in Donegal.

Captain Charles J. McGuinness – © www.SailorofFortune.com

Charlie was described as a swashbuckler to the manor born. Slightly over middle height and sturdily built, he walked with a swagger and, onshore he invariably wore a black trench coat and a black trilby hat. It seemed as though it was his intention to display himself, to trail his coat, as it were, and to provoke the RIC and Black and Tans into some action against him. It was a dangerous way to go about in dangerous times.

Frank Carty later recalled that "while in Derry Jail I was confined in a hospital ward on the second floor. The hospital ward was about 22 feet from the outer wall of the prison alongside Harding Street. The sill of the window in the ward was about level with the top of the outer wall. The window on the outside was protected by 1 ¾ " square iron bars which were set about 6 inches apart. Early in January I succeeded in smuggling out a plan to the O.C. in Derry for my escape. My plan was briefly to be supplied with a hack saw and a supply of blades to enable me to cut one of the bars; then my escape depended upon cooperation from outside at a date and time to be fixed. My plan reached Frank Carney TD who was then in charge of the Derry area. By him they were communicated to Captain C. McGuinness."[5]

Towards the end of January McGuinness sent word to Carty, through a friendly warder, that he would make the attempt at about 4.30 on the morning of Saturday 12 February. As a first step he had a hacksaw smuggled in to him, then a message that it was essential for him to be in the hospital block at the back of the jail yard, abutting on Harding Street, at the time of the attempt. Carty's wound had healed, though the wrist still troubled him and was stiff, but it was not bad enough to warrant the prison doctor having him transferred to the hospital. So Carty worked the old army dodge of a pain in the back. It took days and nights of acting before he finally convinced the doctor that he was a hospital case.

McGuinness, having got word that Carty was in the right place to saw through the bars in his cell window in the hospital, would himself gain entry into the backyard of one of the little houses in Harding Street, scale the wall and throw a rope ladder to the prisoner.

In his book *Nomad*, McGuinness describes the abortive attempt as follows:

41

"The coil of rope, fastened with a steel hook to grip the top of the wall, was in readiness - also the silk ladder to bridge the gap between cell window and wall.

At four o'clock, I ascended the roof of an outhouse directly under the (forty foot) wall nearest to Carty's hospital cell. I coiled the rope carefully, taking care not to offer an exposed silhouette to any vigilant eye. The streets were lined with sandbag barricades and (British Army) machine-gun emplacements. Any moving shadow became an immediate target.

Satisfied that all was clear, I heaved the rope. The hook missed the wall coping by a foot, and clattered down with a horrible din, echoes rumbling throughout the yards. Prepared for the worst, I cocked my gun and waited - one minute, five minutes, ten minutes. But nothing happened! Again I coiled the rope, measuring for distance carefully. This time my efforts were successful and the hook gripped the top of the parapet.

Up the rope I scrambled, the silk ladder coiled around my waist. Then came a further misfortune. I had scarcely climbed ten feet when a piece of old coping stone broke loose under my weight and the heavy stone tumbled down, missing me by a fraction of a foot."

McGuinness, however, had not given up the attempt. He had merely postponed it. Within hours of that first failure, a friendly warder had smuggled another message, a present of a ball of fisherman's twine. Inside it were instructions on how it was to be used and when. And so it was that at 4.30am, on 15th February 1921, the day he was to be taken before the British court-martial, Frank Carty again stared out through his prison bars, tensely awaiting the signal.

Outside McGuinness was laboriously clambering over the yard walls of the Unionist terrace houses in Harding Street. As the Guildhall clock chimed the half hour Carty heard the low whistle from McGuinness. Tying the end of the twine to the bars he lobbed the bundle up and over the wall. Two quick tugs - the 'all clear' signal - quickly reassured Carty and he tugged back. Below, McGuinness was attaching the thin rope ladder to the twine and Carty was trying to haul it up and over the wall. Once more disaster struck, the ladder snagged on the coping as it reached the top of the wall. With controlled haste, McGuinness drew the ladder down and Carty, fortunately having realised what was happening, slacked the twine, and at the knot he tied a note which explained that as the ladder would continue to foul, it could not be used and that, consequently, Carty must swarm over the rope to clear the fifteen-foot gap between his cell window and the wall. This time the haulage operation was successful and Carty fastened the rope to a sound window-bar. Then he forced his great bulk through the space that opened after he had pushed aside the sawn-through bars. With desperate energy he managed to lever himself painfully along the rope. His wounded wrist was of little use in this operation during which the rope sagged so much under his weight that he had to haul himself almost perpendicularly up the last few feet to the top of the wall.

Somehow he made it. Seconds later the hefty Brigadier was scrambling down the rope ladder into the yard at the back of Moore's house. The pair exchanged whispered greetings, and then they were both climbing the backyard walls of the street of houses until they arrived outside the unoccupied end house. Having entered the house by the backdoor, they slipped out through the front into Harding Street, and through a maze of back streets out of the Orange quarter towards the Strand and comparative safety.

Alert for the booming cannon which would signal the discovery of the escape; they hurried along and fortunately succeeded in avoiding the enemy patrols. Still the cannon did not boom. They were undercover when the escape was discovered and the alarm sounded at 7 o'clock in the morning. The RIC and Military were furious at the successful escape of Carty and they immediately swamped Derry in a search operation.[6]

After remaining in Derry for about eight or ten days Carty crossed in a coal boat to Workington in Cumbria. From there he made his way to Glasgow. According to Carty the IRA were notified of his arrival and he got in touch with them as soon he reached the city. He was in the care of a Doctor Cush for some time and at the end of about six weeks was in perfect health.

Towards the end of April the Assistant Quartermaster General of the IRA, Daniel Patrick Walsh from County Tipperary, was in Glasgow for supplies of munitions. Carty may have already known him, as he sent stuff to Brigadier Pilkington of the Sligo Brigade via Belfast. A coal strike was in progress at the time and Walsh was waiting to get the stuff he had purchased dispatched to Ireland before leaving himself. Carty states that, "I had arranged to accompany D.P. Walsh to Dublin and was waiting until he would be ready to leave".[7]

Frank Carty was staying with a local IRA Volunteer, Frank O'Hagan, in the Gorbals, but the Glasgow police were already on his trail. The Irish districts of the city became suspect and were kept under surveillance. On April 28 they raided the house of Republican sympathisers in Shawlands called McEnearney, and whilst there they found two letters in envelopes. They were both addressed to "Frank", and the first, which purported to be written by someone called "Jones", started "Dear Frank; it said, "I suppose you are having a high old time there; God knows you need it after so many dreary months...I don't think the police have given up hope, so you will have to exercise the greatest caution when attempting to come back". In the other letter, which was from "Cissie", was the sentence, "You will need to be careful and to watch yourself". No explanation was received as to how the letters came to be there.[8]

The police were on the lookout for Carty and another man wanted in Ireland, and after the raid on the McEnearneys, they went to O'Hagan's house at 69 Abbotsford Place. There they found Carty lying in bed and when asked his name, he gave them the alias of Frank Somers. They believed he was one of the men they were looking for. At the time the police knew that the man they wanted was charged with prison-breaking and robbery, but afterwards learned that there was also a charge of murder against him.

44

He appeared before the Central District Court in St Andrews Square and was remanded until May 4. The Glasgow IRA knew that it would only be a matter of time before Carty's real identity was discovered by the authorities, and so they set about making plans to rescue him for the third time. There was no hope of getting him over the walls of Duke Street Prison, they believed, the jail being in the heart of the city and the warders were tough and loyal. The local IRA were soon putting together a daring rescue plan.

Notes

1. As General Perceval, he surrendered Singapore to the Japanese without firing a shot in 1942.
2. This account of the freeing of Carty is substantially based on 'Rescue of Frank Carty from Sligo Jail' by Billy Kelly, in *Sworn to Be Free: The Complete Book of IRA Jailbreaks, 1918-1921*, (ed. Florence O'Donoghue) Anvil, Tralee, 1971, pp.108-115.
3. Michael Farry, *Sligo 1914-1921: A Chronicle of Conflict*, Killoran Press, Trim, County Meath, 1992, p.203.
4. Uinseann Mac Eoin, *Survivors*, Argenta, Dublin, 1987, p.142.
5. Statement of Military Activities of Frank Carty, late O.C. 4th Brigade, 3rd Western Division, 1935, p.16.
6. Accounts of Carty's escape from Derry Jail can be found in *Charles 'Nomad' McGuinness*, by John McGuffin and Joseph Mulheron, Irish Resistance Books, Derry, 2002, pp.50-52; Michael MacUileagoid, *From Fetters to Freedom: The Inside Story of Irish Jailbreaks*, Coloured Books, Belfast, 1996, pp.81-82; Billy Kelly, in *Sworn to Be Free: The Complete Book of IRA Jailbreaks, 1918-1921*, (edited by Florence O'Donoghue) Anvil, Tralee, 1971, pp.122-129.
7. Statement of Military Activities of Frank Carty, late O.C. 4th Brigade, 3rd Western Division, 1935, p17.
8. These letters were productions in the Glasgow Prison Van Case trial.

Chapter 3

Ambush

Following his arrest, Frank Carty was twice remanded in custody at the Central Police Court, the second occasion being on 4th May, when he was committed to Duke Street Prison for four days. It was on the journey from the police court to the prison that the van transporting Carty was ambushed.

The following dramatic account of the attempt to free Frank Carty from the prison van was published in the 5 May 1921 edition of the *Glasgow Herald* newspaper and contains the official police report of what happened. The inside story of the rescue is given in Chapter 7.

"STORY OF THE CRIME

A police motor van on its way to Duke Street Prison was attacked by an armed gang in High Street, Glasgow, shortly after noon yesterday. Inspector Robert Johnston was shot dead and Detective Sergeant George Stirton received a bullet wound in the wrist. Up till a late hour last night 17 men (including it is understood, a priest) and one woman had been arrested. That in brief tells the story of one of the most dastardly outrages in the modern history of Glasgow. Happening in broad daylight in the heart of the city, the murder, associated as it was with a fierce revolver fight between the police and desperadoes created a tremendous sensation in the vicinity, and throughout the west of Scotland as the facts became known. All the circumstances point to the outrage being the work of Sinn Fein sympathisers. In many regards it resembles the Fenian attack on a police van in Manchester in September, 1867, for which the Manchester Martyrs were hanged[1]; and probably not since the Dynamitards made their attempt to blow up Tradeston gasometer in Glasgow in the early eighties has the public been so alarmed and stirred with indignation as it was yesterday.[2]

CAREFULLY PREPARED AMBUSH

The tragedy arose out of an attempt to rescue a prisoner named Frank Somers, alleged to be a wanted man by the Irish police authorities. He appeared for the second time before Stipendiary Neilson at the Central Police Court yesterday morning, and was remanded till Saturday on a charge of having broken out of Sligo Jail in June of last year and out of Derry Jail in February, and also having stolen a revolver in Sligo in November last. When the court proceedings were over he was put into a motor van, which set out to carry him to Duke Street Prison. Whether the police were prompted to take extra precautions has not transpired, but the van was furnished with a strong escort. A second prisoner was in the van, but he was in no way associated with Somers. Each man was put into a separate cabin in the commodious wagon, inside of which travelled two police officers and the two doors forming the end of the vehicle were securely locked. On the seat along with the driver, Constable Thomas Ross, were three officers - Inspector Robert Johnston, Detective Sergeant Stirton, and Detective Constable MacDonald. Johnston occupied the end position, having his left leg over the edge his foot resting on the footboard. The van left the courtyard of the Central Police Station in St Andrews Square at ten minutes past twelve noon. Within five minutes it had climbed the steep gradient in High Street, and when at the historic Bell o' the Brae it ran into what appears to have been a carefully prepared ambush.[3] The spot was well chosen. On the right hand side of the street is bounded by the high wall of the prison, and on the left by the Corporation Water Pumping Station, so that there are no windows from which suspicious movements could be clearly observed.[4] The route to the prison entrance in Drygate leaves High Street just at the steepest part of the incline, and it was here the assailants planned to attack rightly judging that the motor would be slowed down as the driver changed gear preparatory to turning into Drygate. The assailants were divided into three gangs each, so far as can be learned consisting of from ten to a dozen men.

This composite picture illustrates the scene at the time of the ambush. The position of the police van and direction from which the IRA fired are clearly defined.

FIERCE REVOLVER FIGHT

When the van was slowing down opposite the pumping station the gangs attacked simultaneously, completely taking the officers by surprise. One company emerged from Rotten Row. A second advanced from the south-west corner of Cathedral Square, and the third came up at the rear of the van. The first shots came from the rear, and before the police party could investigate fire was opened from the front and flank. Almost simultaneously Inspector Johnston fell from his seat, shot through the heart. He rolled on to the roadway, and expired immediately afterwards. The van, as the driver changed gear, came to a stop. Sergeant Stirton with great courage jumped from his seat and stood over the body of his fallen comrade. Drawing his revolver he fired at the assailants who appeared to be closing in on the van, firing as they did so. Before he could set off another shot he was struck by a bullet in the right wrist, which incapacitated him from further using his weapon. He stood his ground, however, and was pluckily supported by his colleagues. Detective MacDonald in his place had also drawn his revolver, and for several seconds a fierce fight took place. Bullets rattled against the prison wall, leaving marks in the

48

masonry. Three shots pierced the radiator of the motor; one went through the mud screen, and several through the windscreen, the glass of which crashed in on the dashboard. The object of the front and flank attack had obviously been to hold the attention of the officers while the rear gang of assailants should release the prisoner.

This photograph was taken from the spot where the IRA active service unit closed in, the dotted line showing the course of the prison van as it approached them. A stray bullet went through the window of the Hydraulic Pumping Station (marked by a white cross) opposite.

FOILED RESCUERS

The attackers had evidently came close up to the back of the van, and had either inserted the muzzles of their revolvers into the key holes of the two doors or scored chance "bulls" for two bullets were fired into the locks, the intention being to open the door and to rescue Somers. The locks were destroyed but the doors held, and the plans of the would-be rescuers failed. The officers and prisoners inside were not free from danger. In addition to the shots which damaged the locks, a bullet pierced the door and went whizzing through the interior crushing against the boards behind the driver's seat. The officers were unable to get out because of the damaged doors laid down on the floor, a precaution that was also taken by one of the prisoners, and they remained till the firing ceased. The plucky fight put up by the officers in front caused the miscreants to draw off, and within minutes of the opening of the attack they had scattered and disappeared along the various streets leading from the Square. A private motor came up High Street, and without delay Inspector Johnston's body and the wounded officer Stirton were conveyed to the Royal Infirmary. Constable Ross meanwhile started his motor, and in a few seconds the prison gate was reached, and when the van had passed inside, the damaged doors were forced open and the prisoners accompanied by their escort (Constables George Bernard and Assistant Court Officer David Brown), entered the building.

The rear of the police van showing a bullet-hole in the lock and the splintered panelling.

MEN NOTICED BY PATROL

It appears that there was very little traffic on the street in the immediate vicinity at the time the outrage was committed, and few people actually saw the attack being delivered. At the point at which it occurred the scene would not come quite within the range of vision of pedestrians in the section of High Street which flanks Cathedral Street, nor would it be observable from the square itself, except from a small portion of the open space. The view is obstructed on the one side by the buildings at the end of Rottenrow, and on the other side by the wall which surrounds the prison. In the vicinity of the square unemployed men frequently foregather, and the presence of an idle group would not seriously attract any attention. The movements of the armed civilians preparatory to the attack evidently aroused no suspicion among the ordinary passers-by, although two armed constables who were on patrol duty outside the prison noted their presence. The patrol passed on, and at the time of the attack they were some distance along High Street. So sudden and brief was the encounter that even near spectators did not appreciate what was happening. The general impression at first was that the exhaust of a motor car caused the explosions. When it was realised that revolvers were being used the few persons who were about – and these included several children who were on their way to school at the midday interval – were alarmed and ran for shelter to the nearest shops and houses. In the excitement and confusion probably no one had more than a glimpse of the mimic battle which raged for a brief space.

According to the story of eyewitnesses, the attackers failing in their attempt to smash the lock of the van immediately tried to make good their escape. They fled in different directions. A party composed of it was estimated of about 10 men, ran along the Rottenrow, with Detective Sergeant Stirton injured though he was pursuing them for a short distance. Another party of men, three in number, rushed along the Drygate, revolvers in their hands, and turned into the square. They proceeded thence towards Castle Street, and shoving the revolvers in their pockets as they were crossing the square, and, appearing to recover their composure, they mixed with the people who were walking along Castle Street."

The scene of the ambush looking from Rottenrow. Inset, Inspector Johnston.

The spot at which the van halted.   *Constable Bernard.*   *Bullet mark in wall.*

THE POLICE REPORT

The official report by the police is as follows:- Detective Constable MacDonald reports that at 12.15pm today, while escorting a patrol wagon to Duke Street Prison with Frank Somers, charged with theft and prison breaking in Ireland, and another charged with indecent assault, who were under an escort comprising Detective Sergeant George Stirton, and Constables David Brown and George Bernard, an attack was made upon the escort. When the wagon was passing the pumping station in High Street near the corner of Rottenrow three parties of armed men suddenly made their appearance, one at the corner of Rottenrow, one at the south-west corner of Cathedral Square, and the other in the rear immediately started firing. Driver Thomas Ross had occasion at this point to change the gear for the purpose of turning into the prison when the wagon stopped. Inspector Johnston, who was in charge of the escort and occupied a seat to the left of the driver, was shot through the heart on the first discharge of shots. He fell off the wagon onto the roadway, and almost immediately expired. Detective Sergeant Stirton jumped from the front of the wagon and standing across the body of the inspector, discharged the revolver at the assailants.

He had fired only one shot when he received a bullet through the right wrist, and was thus incapacitated from firing. Detective Constable MacDonald, who also occupied a seat on the front of the wagon, emptied his revolver at the assailants on the left and those at the corner of the prison wall. There are several bullet marks on the wagon. Three have pierced the radiator; one went through the mud-screen, and several through the wind-screen. A bullet had been fired into both locks of the doors of the wagon, and a couple of shots had been fired into the offside of the wagon below the driver's seat."

*One of the automatics with which a number of the officers
accompanying the prison van were armed.*

Word of the drama was to reach Glaswegians some hours later
when the three evening papers, the *Times*, *News* and *Citizen*
splashed news of the sensation, some calling it 'The Glasgow
Outrage', others 'The Glasgow Atrocity'. The description of what had
so dramatically occurred was given in full, under such subheadings
as 'Grim Fight under Shadow of Gallows'.

*Constable Thomas Ross the driver is seen with the bullet-riddled
police van. Several shots pierced the radiator, and the windscreen
was smashed.*

54

The War of Independence was avidly reported in the Scottish press. The *Glasgow Herald* was politically hostile to Sinn Féin but the *Scotsman* took so vehemently a pro-Government line that it appeared in some instances to be ahead of the Government itself. The Catholic press, especially the *Glasgow Observer* was sympathetic to the Irish cause based on the fact that Sinn Féin had won an impressive triumph in 1918. Ireland had voted for a 32 county republic and only the Irish people had the right to revoke the decision. The paper contended that anybody who considered them self to be an Irish patriot could not oppose the expressed will of the Irish people. The radical press such as *Forward* were generally sympathetic to Irish aspirations viewing their struggle as anti imperialist.

THE GLASGOW OUTRAGE.
The Bailie - "Ma Conscience! Is this Anno Domini 1715 or the year o' grace 1921?"

The newspaper reports, whilst diverging in some particulars, are substantially identical. Press accounts differ as to the effect of the fusillade on the door of the van. The *Daily Record* says that one of the assailants, "more daring than his fellows, ran into the roadway behind the van just before it started off. Pointing its pistol at the doorway he fired a shot at the lock, the door sprung open." However, as the *Glasgow Herald* correctly reports, "the locks were destroyed but the doors held and the plans of the would-be rescuers failed".

Several newspapers detailed the careers of the wounded policeman and his deceased colleague. Police Inspector Johnston was 41 years of age and was married with two children. He was a native of Castle Douglas, and joined the Glasgow police in 1902. For several years he served in the Eastern Division, where he held the rank of sergeant and was in charge of the organisation of the special constables of the division during the war. Two years before his death he was promoted inspector, and was appointed court officer at the Central Division. His duties there included the calling of the cases in the court and generally the handing over of the prisoners to the officials at Duke Street Prison. Inspector Johnston resided in Shettleston.

Inspector Robert Johnston.

56

Detective Sergeant Stirton was aged 35 and a native of Dundee. He joined the Glasgow police in 1906. He was posted to several divisions before being posted to Central Division. He eventually rose to the rank of Detective Lieutenant. He enlisted in the Army in 1914 and served in the Tank Corps attaining the rank of Sergeant Major. He was also awarded the D.C.M. and M.S.S. for gallantry in action.[5]

Detective Sergeant George Stirton.

The rescue attempt was just one of many actions carried out by the IRA during this period. The Anglo-Irish War was raging and there were daily battles between Republicans and the Crown forces. In the greatest operation in the West of Ireland in the War of Independence, a successful ambush against superior British forces in Tourmakeady, County Mayo on the 3rd of May, resulted in ten British soldiers' casualties against two IRA losses.[6] On the day of the Glasgow ambush there had been a spectacular and deadly ambush of a nine-man RIC patrol in County Kerry when only one officer survived.

This was also a time of industrial unrest throughout Britain and in Glasgow there were strikes in the docks and on the tramcars. Crews of ships, gas supply workers and railwaymen were all on strike, and on the day of the rescue bid, it was the 27th day of a miner's strike.[7]

The next chapter shall describe the aftermath of the ambush.

57

Notes

1. On 18 September 1867 Thomas Kelly and Timothy Deasy, two leading Fenians, were being transported from the courthouse in Manchester to the county jail when the police van containing them was attacked. The prisoners escaped, but an unarmed police sergeant was shot dead. Twenty-nine arrests followed, and in November five men were convicted of murder. One was subsequently pardoned and another's sentence was commuted, but three men, William O'Meara Allen, Michael Larkin, and William O'Brien were hanged. The rescue attempt is also known as the Smashing of the Van.
2. The American based Skirmisher and Clan na Gael movements carried out the bombings in Glasgow, London and Liverpool.
3. Glasgow's first battle is supposed to have taken place at the Bell o' the Brae. Around 1297 there was an English garrison in the Bishops Castle at the top of High Street. Sir William Wallace, Liberator of the Scots, attacked the castle and the English chased him down High Street, but just there, as planned, the Scots turned to fight. Another Scottish force, led by Wallace's uncle, Auchinleck, came up the Drygate and attacked from the rear. The English hemmed in back and front were defeated. Some cast doubt on the authenticity of this tale which was recorded by the poet Blind Harry in the 15th century. The Bell o' the Brae was the scene of another skirmish in 1606 between the Stewarts of Minto and Sir George Elphinstoun, the provost, and five archers who were attacked when returning from archery practice at the City butts at Barrowfield. They defended themselves but as the Stewarts numbered 300, Sir George was compelled to seek the protection of the Earl of Wigton, whose mansion or fortalice was in the High Street. For this "riot", as it was called, the Privy Council punished the ringleaders by imprisonment.
4. On the site of the Hydraulic Pumping Station once stood the drugstore of Dr. Thomas Lyle, the author of the song 'Kelvingrove' which starts 'Will ye gang to Kelvingrove, bonnie lassie, O?
5. Inspector Robert Johnston and D.S. Stirton's war medals are on display in the Glasgow Police Museum in Turnbull Street.
6. For an account of the Tourmakeady ambush see *Dilseacht: The Story of Comdt. General Tom Maguire and the Second (All-Ireland) Dáil*, Ruairi Ó Brádaigh, Elo Press Ltd, Dublin, 1997.
7. John Burrowes, 'The Glasgow Outrage' in *Great Glasgow Stories*, Mainstream Publishing, Edinburgh, 1998, p.148.

Chapter 4

Aftermath

The Chief Constable of Glasgow, James Stevenson, was determined to bring those responsible for the ambush to book. A native of Athlone in County Westmeath, Stevenson joined the RIC in 1884 and rose to the rank of District Inspector in Belfast, at a time of considerable unrest in the city. He was heavily involved in the "Bloody Friday" riot in George Square in 1919 and many critics blamed him for starting the riots when he ordered his men to clear the streets.[1]

In a letter dated 4th May 1921, sent to the Under Secretary for Scotland, Stevenson gives a concise report of the ambush and states that "in view of the possibility of an attempted rescue, a strong escort was placed on the van".[2]

Arrests

The police wasted no time in trying to investigate the attack on the van and the killing of their colleague. They concentrated their efforts on districts which housed the majority of the city's Irish community, and within a few hours many people with known Sinn Féin connections were apprehended.

One of those arrested was the Rev. Patrick MacRory, a young curate at St Mary's, Abercromby Street in the Calton. When the detectives visited the Presbytery to arrest him, news of the visit spread rapidly in the neighbourhood, and large crowds assembled round the house. Presently the detectives emerged accompanied by the parish priest, Father Fitzgerald, and Father MacRory. It was stated that only Father MacRory was under arrest, and that Father Fitzgerald was merely accompanying his curate to the police office in Tobago Street. Popular resentment was freely expressed and a reported two thousand people gathered on the streets and missiles were thrown at the police who drew their batons to ward off attacks.

One of several tramcars attacked in the Gallowgate following the arrest of Father MacRory.

The position seemed so grave on the night of the ambush that a detachment of Gordon Highlanders wearing steel helmets and carrying fixed bayonets was brought from Maryhill Barracks to assist the police to cope with the rioting. Five other arrests were made in the same street and excitement prevailed until a late hour, a passing tramcar being attacked on its way through Abercromby Street. The windows of ten shops were smashed in the Gallowgate. The streets were eventually cleared, Father Fitzgerald having appealed to the people to disperse, but for some time there continued to be great excitement in the district. A military guard was placed on the police station.

This wasn't the first time that the ordinary people of the Calton came face to face with military might. In what has been regarded as the first generation of Red Clydesiders, six weavers were slaughtered and many others wounded by the Dorset Militia in 1787, when they dared to demonstrate for the right to work and a living wage.[3]

St Mary's Parish had a large Irish population and in the crypt of the Church are buried five Irish priests who died in 1847 of the prevailing

60

epidemic of fever. For many years there existed a district in the Calton known as "Connacht Square" by the people of Glasgow because it continued the language and traditions of the west of Ireland.[4]

Father Patrick MacRory

The newspapers reported that, at the Eastern Police Court, eight men and four women were remanded in connection with the disturbance in Abercromby Street, which followed Father MacRory's arrest. A statement printed in an evening paper of Thursday and alleging that the police entered the church during service while two priests were in the Confessional boxes was denied. The police went straight to the sacristy and to the Priests House.

Prisoners Remanded

On the 5th May the arrested prisoners were brought before Stipendiary Neilson at Glasgow Central Police Court and formally charged. They were of various ages ranging from 19 to 58 years.

Nearly all bore Irish names and twelve of the twenty, it was disclosed on the charge sheet, were born in Ireland. The majority of the prisoners were clearly of the manual working class, but several of them had a refined appearance. Almost without exception they were described as being very alert and intelligent. There were a total of twenty prisoners in all, their names being Sean O'Daire (19), James Fullerton (22), Bernard Cunningham (47), Rev. Patrick MacRory (26), Thomas Tracey (45), Mary Tracey (17), Francis O'Hagan (38), Mary McEnearney (36), Alice McEnearney (39), Elizabeth McEnearney (41), William Fullerton (25), Annie Murray (27), Patrick Campbell (38), Michael O'Carroll (19), John McGarrigle (26), Vincent Campbell (20), James McCarra (25), James Mitchell (28), Charles Grier (36), Jane Campbell (26). The three McEnearneys were sisters and the Traceys were husband and wife.

Against the six first named prisoners the charge preferred was: –

"Having on the 4th of May, 1921, while acting in concert with a number of persons at present unknown in High Street, near Drygate, both in Glasgow, discharged loaded firearms at a police patrol van then conveying prisoners to Duke Street Prison, whereby R. Johnston, Police Inspector, Glasgow Police, was fatally wounded and Detective Sergeant G. Stirton, Glasgow Police was wounded in the right arm."

Against the second group: John McGarrigle, Vincent Campbell, James McCarra, James Mitchell, Charles Grier, Jane Campbell, the same charge was read with the following addition: –

"And further with having been found in a house at 74 Abercromby Street in possession of revolvers and ammunition, contrary to the Firearms Act, 1920."

Against the third group comprising: Francis O'Hagan, Mary McEnearney, Alice McEnearney, Elizabeth McEnearney, William Fullerton, Annie Murray, Patrick Campbell, Michael O'Carroll, the charge stated was: –

"Having on the 4th of May, 1921, while acting in concert with a number of persons at present in custody, in High Street, near Drygate, both in Glasgow, discharged loaded firearms at a police patrol van then conveying prisoners to Duke Street Prison, whereby R. Johnston, Police Inspector, Glasgow Police, was fatally wounded and Detective Sergeant G. Stirton, Glasgow Police was wounded in the right arm."

The arms referred to in one of the charges, was the discovery in a cellar of the largest haul of IRA arms and explosives ever found in Glasgow. There were thirty five revolvers, six hand-grenades, a bomb, many pounds of gelignite, a large number of detonators, eight bags of percussion caps, 955 rounds of revolver and rifle ammunition, holsters, magazines, a bayonet, and a coil of fuse wire.

Application was made on behalf of the police that the prisoners be remanded until Saturday, May 7th. The application not being opposed, Stipendiary Neilson granted the remand. None of the prisoners had representation from a solicitor.

The prisoners were held behind the grim walls of Duke Street Prison where conditions were notoriously poor with chronic overcrowding. During this period a range of political prisoners including suffragettes, socialists, anarchists and Irish Republicans were sent to the prison. Some went on hunger strike to protest their treatment. Executions of ordinary prisoners were carried out in the prison from 1865 to 1928.

The forbidding building at Duke Street Prison with exercise ground in front, photographed in 1909.

63

At the Eastern Police Court twelve people were charged with forming part of a riotous crowd and conducting themselves in a disorderly manner the previous night following the arrest of Father MacRory.

The fact that the detectives who were escorting Carty to Duke Street Prison carried revolvers seems to have given rise to the mistaken impression that all police officers were now armed, and it was officially stated that the 4th May was the first time for many years on which any police official accompanying a prison van had been furnished with firearms. Evidently the police were taking no chances with Frank Carty given his two previous jailbreaks and his high-ranking position in the IRA.

The authorities would appear to have seized on the rescue attempt as an excuse for repressive measures against the more advanced sections of the labour movement. The premises of the Scottish Labour College in St Vincent Street were raided at midnight on the 4th May, but nothing incriminating was found. The following day, Tom Mitchell, secretary of the Socialist Labour Party and editor of *The Socialist* was arrested and charged with writing a seditious article. This was possibly revenge for the fact that the Socialist Labour Press printed the Sinn Féin newspaper *Dark Rosaleen*. John MacLean commented, "Underneath lies the idea that a Bolshevik plot is still brewing, and that we communists are linked up with the Sinn Feiners". That Thursday, MacLean addressed a huge meeting at Barrhead where he referred to the death of the police inspector. He counselled Irishmen and Scottish workers not to resort to violence but, "to calmly watch the developments. This is no plea for passive inactivity but for refusal to resort to childish displays of petty force when the Government is ready to give us a deluge of blood".[5]

The newspaper of the Independent Labour Party, *Forward*, endorsed the view expressed in the *Glasgow Observer* that the killing of Inspector Johnston poisoned host-immigrant relations and failed to advance the cause the Republicans sought to promote. It stated that the result was:

> "The immediate interruption again of that cursed anti-Irish, or rather anti-Catholic prejudice, which has for a hundred years kept the working class split into sections and which only in the last decade have we got partially smothered. And not only that, but the growing sympathies of the Protestant and

other non-Catholic workers for the Irish people under the vicious Greenwood George terror have suddenly withered. You can hear the anti-Sinn Fein rumble in every hand; and as in England, the burning of farmstacks, warehouses, and hotel bedrooms by alleged Sinn Feiners, has resulted in the strengthening of the reactionary forces there, so too will it be in Scotland. "[6]

The newspapers reported that Inspector Johnston's funeral took place on 7th May. After a service at Shettleston, the coffin containing his body was conveyed to his native Castle Douglas. The mourners included the Lord Provost and other representatives of the Corporation, the Chief Constable, J.V. Stevenson, and members of several police forces including a contingent from the RIC. The *Glasgow Herald* stated that, "on the part of the general public the funeral procession through the streets of the city was the occasion for a striking tribute of sympathy".

On The 7th of May armed members of the RIC escorted Frank Carty to Holyhead, where he was placed on board a naval vessel and taken to Dublin where he was placed in Mountjoy Jail.

In what was described as a sensational sequel to the ambush, the *Glasgow Herald* on 9th May reported that the Chief Constable was sent two letters of a threatening and intimidating character towards the police. They purported to have been sent by the IRA and Sinn Féin and to make references to the arrest of Fr. MacRory and demanded his release. It is unlikely, however, that either of the handwritten letters came from the sources claimed. One is signed "President of the Council of the Irish Republican Army" which was a non-existent designation. It is more than likely that some enraged individual who believed the false rumour that the police entered the Chapel of St Mary's to arrest Father MacRory composed the letters.

Father MacRory who was a native of Deerpark, in Omagh in County Tyrone, was by all accounts a very popular young priest. His first curacy, which was to be his only pastoral charge, was St Mary's where he had served for less than two years before his arrest.

65

Father Patrick MacRory

During the detention of Father MacRory, the *Glasgow Observer* commented on the "unprecedented feeling" aroused by the young priest's arrest:

> "His arrest and detention have aroused an unprecedented feeling in Eastern Glasgow, and the utmost sympathy has been manifested by the people of St Mary's in the best possible way - by intercession to the Almighty for the young priest's speedy release.

> The all-night vigil in St Mary's Church on Tuesday night was one of the most remarkable religious services in the record of the Church in Scotland. It began practically without any preparation or announcement but the news that it was to take place got around the Parish like wildfire and before midnight the church was packed to the door. Confessions were heard during the night by the clergy of the Parish assisted by other priests from neighbouring missions and the numbers of communicants at the morning Mass were enormous.

> In the experience of all the priests assisting, the fervour of the congregation surpassed any witnessed even at the

mission services in the Parish. At midnight Stations of the Cross took place and a special service followed every hour during the night conducted mainly by Rev. Dr. McEwan, other priests remaining in the confessionals, which were thronged with penitents."

The article went on to state:

"If a plebiscite of Glasgow Catholics were taken to decide who, at present, is the city's most popular clergyman, there can be no doubt that the choice would fall upon Rev. Patrick MacRory of St Mary's.....and his warmest advocates would be his fellow clergy. Indeed it is highly probable that not a single vote would be cast elsewhere - that Father MacRory would have a walkover.

Until a few weeks ago this young priest was practically unknown. Today his name is on everyone's lips and his welfare is the burden of thousands of prayers offered on his behalf by the faithful Irish Catholic people of Scotland's greatest city...

By what means has he attained such unparalleled popularity?....His fame is not of his own seeking, for there is no more modest, retiring, pious and hard working priest to be found anywhere. But like the overwhelming majority of Glasgow Irish people, he has Sinn Fein sympathies, also he assiduously visits the Catholic families in his district...To these two circumstances mainly he owes the fact that he is at present the occupant of a cell in Duke Street Prison and the white headed boy of his co-religionists in the city. He is ever in their thoughts."

While detained in Duke Street Prison, Father Pat, as his parishioners affectionately knew him, wrote home to his mother, and the letter, dated 18th July 1921 has been carefully preserved in the family homestead. He wrote about his hopes of being released, about letters he had had from his mother, brother and friends. He asks his mother, "If you have time you might send a sheet of notepaper, a stamped addressed envelope, a pen and ink to Minnie (his sister). If there is not a shortage of the above items in Knockroe then I can't account for her silence". Some further inquiries about the family and

67

weather are made in the letter before turning to the Truce and the negotiations between the Irish Government and Lloyd George's Cabinet. Fr. Pat asks, "What do you think of the prospects of peace in Ireland. Things look hopeful - more hopeful than they did for a long time. It does seem that the B. Government are in earnest about it. The Truce and the implied recognition of the I.R.A. show that. Everyone would be glad if something comes from the present conferences. There was a Tridium in St Mary's last week for that intention".[7]

Father MacRory had his morale lifted in prison by friends telling him stories of great Glasgow Celtic players like Sandy McMahon, Jimmy Quinn and Patsy Gallagher. He must have been proud that his beloved Celtic was founded in the parish hall of St Mary's to raise money for the poor of the East End thirty-three years earlier.[8] It was also said that the Rory O'Moore Flute Band played Irish airs outside the prison to raise his spirits. Fr. MacRory is supposed to have acknowledged this show of support by waving a green handkerchief from his cell window.[9]

Further arrests were made in the days following the ambush. These included James Kavanagh (22), Thomas Docherty (26), Joseph Shields senior (52) and Joseph Shields junior (19), Thomas Fenton (21), John Carney (54), Thomas Hickey (22), Margaret Dehan or Quinn (18), Thomas Moorhead (20), Patrick Keenan (23), John Gallagher, Thomas Curtin, Michael Duggan, and Eugene Duggan. The 19th May edition of the *Glasgow Herald* reported that the total number of people held in custody in connection with the rescue attempt was 32. Thomas Moorhead and Patrick Keenan were released soon afterwards.

Fr. MacRory made an application for permission meet with his superior, Fr Fitzgerald, in connection to matters relating to the parish. The Stipendiary refused the request.

There were more arrests before the end of May and these included Matthew Tipping (32), James McCann (24), Seámus Reader (23) and Andrew Fagan (26). Some of the prisoners were freed including John Leonard (27) who was only briefly held, and three young men from the Hillhead district of the city whose names were Thomas Curtin, Michael Duggan and Eugene Duggan.

The Chief Constable was dealt a serious personal blow when his son DI Stevenson of the RIC was one of six British forces killed in an IRA ambush on 3rd June at Carrowkennedy in County Mayo.[10]

There was no let-up in the police investigation and the arrest of James Sherry (57) in June was to be followed in July by the arrests in Edinburgh of three men whom the police had been keen to detain. They were Seaghan Mooney (18), his brother Éamonn Mooney (22), and Frederick Quinn (21), who it was reported had served in the Gordon Highlanders.

The 23rd July edition of the *Glasgow Herald* announced that arrangements had been completed in connection with the trial of 13 men who were in custody on suspicion of having been concerned in the attack on the police patrol van. The trial was scheduled to start on 8th August and would be conducted in Edinburgh High Court.

> "In the indictment the men were accused of conspiring with other persons to further the objects of Sinn Fein by the unlawful use of force and violence, especially by means of explosives, firearms, etc, to the danger of the lives and property of lieges. They were further charged with conspiring to release from the custody of the police authorities Frank T. Carty, alias Frank Somers, a member of the Irish Republican Army who had been arrested on charges of theft and prison-breaking in Ireland, and who was in custody pending the arrival of officers from Ireland, by breaking into the police patrol van in which he was being conveyed to Duke Street, and by assembling with loaded firearms, and discharging these at Inspector Robert Johnston, Detective-Sergeant Stirton, Detective-Constable Murdoch McDonald, and Thomas Ross, motorman, who were in charge of the van, with intent to murder them and to break into the van, they assaulted the four officers, murdered Inspector-Johnston, and seriously injured Sergeant Stirton to the danger of his life, destroyed the lock of the patrol van attempted to force it open."

It was expected that the trial would last about ten days. There were 21 documentary productions, 129 label productions, and it was anticipated that 138 witnesses would be called for the Crown. The pleading diet in connection with the trial was scheduled to take place in the Judicial Buildings, Jail Square, Glasgow on 29th July.

A 'Defence of Irish Political Prisoners (Scotland) Fund' was created to raise money to pay for the hefty legal costs of the trial and various fundraising events were undertaken. British intelligence sources claimed that the Catholic clergy helped organise a Gaelic fair in the grounds of Kenmure House in Bishopbriggs on June 11th and 12[th.] According to the report about 15,000 attended on the first day and about 20,000 on the second with upwards of £1000 being raised.[11]

Most of those originally charged with offences relating to the ambush were subsequently released. On 22 July, 11 men and 7 women were freed, the case against them having been withdrawn. They were Rev. Patrick MacRory, Joseph Shields senior, Joseph Shields junior, Thomas Fenton, Bernard Cunningham, Thomas Hickey, Patrick Campbell, Thomas Docherty, Andrew Fagan, Matthew Tipping, James McCann, Mary McEnearney, Alice McEnearney, Elizabeth McEnearney, Mary Tracey, Annie Murray, Jane Campbell and Margaret Quinn. A large crowd of well-wishers assembled in the Drygate in order to welcome the released prisoners.

A crowd of several thousand gathered outside St Mary's Church to welcome Father MacRory on his release. "From many windows Irish Republican flags were displayed and near the chapel a green banner stretched across the street bearing the words 'Cead Mille Failte'.' About six o'clock a motorcar conveying Father MacRory, who was accompanied by the Rev. Father Fitzgerald and the Rev. Father McEwan, reached the vicinity of the chapel. An immense crowd surrounded the car and Father MacRory, who had to acknowledge repeated outbursts of cheering, was almost carried from the car to the presbytery house entrance. A number of Irish songs were sung by the demonstrators including 'The Soldier's Song' and 'God Save Ireland," the local press reported.

The *Glasgow Observer* reported on the scenes that greeted Fr. MacRory upon his release from Duke Street Prison:

Father MacRory was the hero of the moment and he was "mobbed" as Father Fitzgerald escorted him to a waiting taxi. A woman who waited all day long in the crush presented Father MacRory with a fine bouquet of flowers.

"From dawn on Friday morning the news seemed to have spread far and wide and Calton joyfully set itself the task of preparing a suitable welcome for its Soggarth Aroon (*beloved priest*). 'Unroll Erin's flag; fling its folds to the breeze! Let it wave o'er the land, let it float to the seas!'

The green, white and gold of Ireland simply obliterates the deep frontages of Abercromby Street and the adjacent network of throughfares; and it was through an avenue of Sinn Fein flags that one approached St Mary's presbytery around which had congregated thousands of Irish people, almost frantic with joyful exuberance at the prospect of welcoming their young priest.

'Cead Mille Failte' was the cheering, welcoming legend on a great banner stretched across Abercromby Street. Myriads of Sinn Fein flags fluttered in the breeze, the heraldic banners of the four provinces floating proudly above the throng. The chapel house was gaily beflagged and from Father MacRory's own window streamed a great Sinn Fein standard with the Red Hand of Ulster on its centre panel. Hundreds of children dressed in green paraded in the street.

For hours the crowd in increasing numbers awaited in Abercromby Street and Gallowgate. The (AOH) band brightened the tedium with lively music while from time to time the children and the people sang patriotic airs, 'God Save Ireland' and 'The Soldier's Song.'

Father MacRory was the first of the released prisoners to appear from the prison gateway in an open car. He received an enthusiastic welcome from the crowd which, numbering several hundred had mustered in the Drygate.

Shortly before six the car conveying Father Fitzgerald and Father MacRory was seen by thousands in Abercromby Street. The scene of welcome defies description. He was carried down from the car to the presbytery. A baby girl brought for baptism in St Mary's on that Friday was given a name commemorative of the day. She is Elizabeth MacRory O'Reilly."

Father MacRory receives a hero's welcome upon his release from Duke Street Prison.

72

Notes

1. On 31st January 1919 during the 'Forty Hours Strike' the Government dispatched 12,000 troops, 100 lorries and six tanks onto the streets of Glasgow and the Red Flag in George Square had raised the spectre of revolution.
2. The police report and correspondence concerning the attack on the prison van is contained in a file titled 'Irish Disturbances' (ref HH055/00063) in the National Archives of Scotland. The file was opened in 1994 although the information on the van episode was not technically due for release until 2023.
3. For an account of the strike see *The Strike of the Calton Weavers 1787* by Elspeth King, Glasgow Museums and Art Galleries, 1987.
4. See *St Mary's, Glasgow, 1842-1942*, Centenary Souvenir, 1942.
5. Nan Milton, *John MacLean: In the Rapids of Revolution,* Allison and Busby Ltd, London, 1978, p.229-232.
6. *Forward*, 14 May 1921.
7. I am grateful to Colm MacRory, a nephew of Fr. MacRory, for supplying me with this information.
8. Potter, David W., *The Life and Times of Patsy Gallagher*, Parrs Ward Press, Manchester, 2000, p.78.
9. Related to me by the late Frank McGowan, Glasgow.
10. Hopkinson, Michael, *The Irish War of Independence*, Gill & McMillan, Dublin, 2004, p.135.
11. Report on the Activities of Revolutionary Organisations in the United Kingdom. CP3055 1 June 1921; CP 3074 23 June 1921, Cab 24/125.

Chapter 5

Trial

The 13 men who were charged attended a pleading diet on 29 July in the Judiciary Buildings in Jail Square in Glasgow.

When the court officer read the names of the prisoners they arose from their seats. As each name was read it was customary for prisoners to respond with "Here" or "Present". The first two replied with "Here", but the third and several others after him responded in Irish Gaelic. This brought a smile to the faces of most of the prisoners.

Sheriff Fyfe, addressing the prisoners, said, "You are all charged with conspiracy to endanger life and destroy property, with murder, and with shooting to the danger of life, all of which is set forth in the indictment which has been served on each of you". He then asked if they desired to plead "guilty" or "not guilty". Each in turn pleaded "not guilty".

The special defence of alibi was tendered on behalf of each of the prisoners. The Procurator-Fiscal (Mr Strathern) held that the special defence in two of the cases was too vague in its terms and was not sufficient to support a special defence of alibi, and he informed the agent that he would require to make the statement more specific in the interest of his clients or they might be shut out in their special defence.

The agents representing the prisoners were – Neil Doherty (for Branniff, O'Daire, and the two Fullertons. McCarra, Kavanagh, and Walsh); Bernard Caufield (for Tracey, O'Hagan, O'Carroll, and Carney); W G Leenihan (for Vincent Campbell); and John Snodgrass (for McGarrigle).

The remainder of this chapter is taken verbatim from the detailed reports of the trial that appeared in the 13th, 20th and 27th of August editions of the *Glasgow Observer*.

"The Case for the Prosecution Presented

Thirteen men are at present on trial for their lives before the High Court, which is sitting in Edinburgh. Their names are Daniel Patrick Walsh alias Joseph Dunne alias James Mitchell, Daniel Branniff alias Charles Grier, James McCarra, John McGarrigle, Vincent Campbell, John Carney, James Fullerton William Fullerton, Michael O'Carroll, Sean O'Daire, James Kavanagh, Thomas Tracey and Francis O'Hagan.

The indictment is wide and sweeping and occupied three pages in print. The thirteen men, it states are accused with having:

(1) In 1920 and 1921 at 171 Renfield Street, Glasgow, known as the James Connolly Sinn Fein Club and Sinn Fein Headquarters in Scotland, and, elsewhere in Glasgow, carried out a conspiracy to further the objects of Sinn Fein by unlawful use of force and violence and especially by means of explosives and firearms to be used for the purpose of endangering the lives and persons and injuring and destroying property.

(2) With having in furtherance of that conspiracy, between 28th April and 5th May, 1921, entered into a conspiracy to release from the custody of the police in Glasgow, Frank T Carty alias Frank Somers, a member of the Irish Republican Army, who had been arrested on charges of theft and prison breaking in Ireland, and who was being detained pending the arrival of officers from Ireland, and thereby murdering the officers in charge of the patrol van in which Carty was to be conveyed from the Central Police Chambers, Glasgow, to the prison of Glasgow, and by breaking into the van, and with having at High Street, Rottenrow, Cathedral Square, and Drygate, Glasgow, on 4th May, assembled, armed with loaded firearms, and discharged them at Robert Johnston, inspector; George C Stirton, detective sergeant; Murdoch Macdonald, detective constable, and Thomas Ross, motorman, being the officers in charge of the patrol van, and that with intent to murder these officers and to break into the van, and with having shot and killed Johnston and murdered him, and shot Stirton in the arm and seriously injured him, and destroyed the lock of the van and attempted to force the van open.

75

The case was opened on Monday before the Lord Justice Clerk (Lord Scott-Dickson) and a mixed jury. Eight men and seven women were empanelled.

Much public interest was evinced in the proceedings, but owing to the large number of jurors cited, and the resulting heavy demand on the accommodation in the courtroom, the police, of whom there was a large staff on duty in the vicinity of the court, refused admission to large numbers of the general public.

A large crowd assembled at Parliament Square before the opening of the trial but they were disappointed in their hopes of seeing the arrival of the prisoners. Admission to the square was by pass and the police kept the crowd at a distance.

The prisoners were transported in a large motor van, in which they were all accommodated, with two smaller vans filled with policemen escorting it.

In the court the thirteen pleaded not guilty to the charges.

The prosecution was conducted by the Solicitor-General (Mr C. D Murray) K.C., M.P.), and the Hon. William Watson, K.C., and Lord Kinross, Advocates Depute. Counsel appeared for the defence as

76

follows: – On behalf of Tracey, Carney, and O'Carroll – Mr Sandeman K.C., and Mr James Macdonald; on behalf of Mitchell, Grier, McCarra, William Fullerton, James Fullerton, Sean O'Daire, and Kavanagh, Mr Morrice Mackay K.C., and Mr Macgregor Mitchell on behalf of Vincent Campbell, Mr Aitchison; on behalf of McGarrigle, Mr Russell; and on behalf of O'Hagan, Mr Duffes. There were some 340 productions in the case, including 211 documentary and 129 labelled. The labelled productions included parts of the damaged police patrol van and a large number of revolvers. The witnesses for the crown numbered 138. Many of the prisoners sought to prove an alibi, and cited a large number of persons to give evidence on their behalf.

The first witness for the prosecution called was Andrew Muir, assistant to a firm of Glasgow engineers, who produced a plan of Glasgow streets in and about the vicinity of High Street and Cathedral Square where the shooting took place. Copies of the plans were given to the jury.

Detective-Sergeant Crawford, Glasgow, then produced a series of six photographs of the scene of the occurrence and of the prison van, showing the marks of the bullets.

Lieutenant James Henderson and Constable Alex Slessor were called to prove that none of the accused was registered to keep firearms or explosives.

Detective-Superintendent Keith, Glasgow, stated in the witness box that it was part of his duties to inquire into the Sinn Fein organisation. He had made investigations at various premises to ascertain if firearms were being concealed, and had found documents of the Sinn Fein and of the Irish Republican Army. On April 29 last he had arrested Carty alias Somers in O'Hagan's house in Abbotsford Place. Carty was in bed at the time. He was charged with breaking out of prison in Sligo and Derry, and with having stolen a revolver. He had received information that Carty was a dangerous man who had twice been rescued. Special precautions were necessary in dealing with him. Witness described how the patrol van was strongly guarded when it left the Central Police Chambers to convey Carty to prison. He heard later by telephone that an attack had been made on the van, and he took steps to trace the men concerned.

The witness stated that there were several companies of the IRA in and around Glasgow and there had been considerable drilling from time to time. It was almost impossible to get evidence about drilling because it was done behind locked doors with sentinels posted to watch the police.

Detective-Sergeant Alexander Mowat said that on May 4th along with other police officers, he visited the house occupied by Jane Campbell at 74 Abercromby Street in Glasgow. He saw Grier, McCarra, Mitchell, McGarrigle and Vincent Campbell. In the presence of those accused witness and the other officers proceeded to make a search of the room. Witness detailed the articles found and now produced. One of these, found on the floor, was a note as follows: – "Wednesday evening, May 4. To D.P. There will be a meeting of P.U.R. Committee tomorrow evening (Thursday), May 5, in same place as last Sunday's meeting was held at 7pm." The note was signed "Grier" and there was also the following postscript: – "If I fail to see you tonight leave a note at your late digs saying what time we are to see you tomorrow." On the floor between the fireplace and the piano a revolver loaded with six cartridges was found. Inside a notebook, which also fell into police hands during the search, were a number of papers, including a note as follows: – "To D.P. If anything is to be done for our friend 'C' tomorrow it will be necessary to see about the matter today. I was here last night and at your digs this morning for five minutes after your departure. I will call at Bridgeton tonight between 10 and 11 on my way home. If you are not there, leave word where you will be found." The note was signed "Grier." Another paper bore the following: "Corner of Rottenrow, 10am. Twenty-five men to be on duty at 10am. O.C.S.B. to meet D at 9am." The witness interpreted O.C.S.B as officer commanding Scottish Brigade.

The witness also stated that he opened a bag and found at Grier's lodgings, and found therein a couple of leaves apparently from a notebook. The first seemed to indicate a visit to a Sinn Fein club. The other bore references to reports, and also the following – "Centre – S Fullerton; subcentre – W Fullerton," and in addition a good deal of information which appeared to be with regard to money transactions.

Cross examined by Mr Mackay, witness admitted that he had read "Dunne" to the jury where "D" was only mentioned in the Rottenrow document. He had been very familiar with the name for the past few months, and it had been a slip on his part. Describing the neighbourhood, witness said that around Abercromby Street there was a very large Irish population, and that the police were taking no chances with anyone.

Mr Mackay – You watched everyone of Irish nationality. Does it come to that!
Witness – No.

Evidence was given by hotel employees regarding five men who had resided at the Ivanhoe Hotel in Buchanan Street, Glasgow, on April 20 and May 1. They could not identify the boarders.

James Malone, a taxi driver whose stance was in St Enoch Square gave evidence regarding a hire by two men whom he drove to Turner Street, and then with two others to 74 Abercromby Street, where one got out, and he drove the others to the Ivanhoe Hotel, Buchanan Street, where two got out. He drove the other man, whom he identified as the prisoner Carney, to 570 Paisley Road West.

The case was then adjourned until the following day (9 August 1921).

When the hearing was resumed the Solicitor-General said he would proceed to consider the afternoon of the 4th May, on the morning of which day the attack occurred.

John MacLean, the boots of the Ivanhoe Hotel, was recalled.

On the 6th May witness was shown from 25 to 30 men and women at the Central Police Station but did not recognise any of them.

The Solicitor-General (indicating the accused) – Do you recognise any of these men as having been in the Ivanhoe Hotel on the morning of 4th May?

Witness – No, sir. I cannot swear by any of them.
Douglas McMillan, a clerk in the employment of Messrs Wylie and Lochhead, said that in the morning of the 4th May he received a telephone message. The voice was that of a woman, who said – "This is Tracey, Parkhead, speaking." Witness knew that Tracey was

an undertaker with whom his firm had had business dealings. It was stated that the motorcar would be used for a considerable part of the day. The order was that it should call at a Buchanan Street hotel, where the driver was to ask for Mr Mitchell. The motorcar returned at 2.45pm and the driver stated he had waited for a considerable time at a certain address. The charge for the car was £2 8s.

Alexander McKechnie, the driver of the car then entered the box. He said that he had driven Mitchell to 74 Abercromby Street. Mitchell went in, came out again alone and was driven to the hotel. He waited for half an hour and then drove Mitchell and another man to Cathedral Street. There they both left the car and went in the direction of Cathedral Square. He afterwards took them to McLeod Street, where the men got out and walked towards Cathedral Square. He waited half an hour and Mitchell appeared with a third man.

He drove to Dale Street, where a young man left the car and returned from Clyde Place with a parcel that witness took to be a small rifle in brown paper. He drove to McLeod Street, where he was asked to wait. His fares walked towards the Square. While waiting there a passer by told him that the prison van had been attacked.

He identified Mitchell and Carney, but could not identify the young man who had carried the parcel.

John Smith, electrical engineer, and Mrs Margaret Grant gave evidence as to the movements of a number of men loitering in High Street and vicinity previous to the occurrence. Smith could not identify any of the accused. Mrs Grant said James McCarra seemed to resemble one of the two men she had seen.

George McCracken, a tramway motorman, said his suspicions had been aroused by seeing an unusual number of men lingering in groups between the corner of Rottenrow and High Street. He called the attention of a policeman to them. Several men were carrying brown paper parcels about 12 inches long. One man who leaned against a wall had beside him a parcel about three feet long. Witness identified McCarra as one of the men he had seen.

Police witnesses identified Carney, Kavanagh and Tracey as men they had seen on the forenoon of May 4 in the vicinity of Cathedral Square and Duke Street Prison.

Evidence was then given by several witnesses regarding the actual attack on the prison van.

Thomas Wallace, a motor driver employed by a Glasgow firm, was the first of these witnesses. He said that about 12.25 on the morning of the 4th he was driving a motor vehicle along High Street to Cathedral Square. The police van was 20 or 30 yards in front of him, and a shot first attracted his attention to it. "It looked," said witness, "as if it was a car with a back-fire." He pulled up his own vehicle just at the back of the police van near the Rottenrow corner, but all he saw of the affair was the inspector falling off the car on to the road. He heard several reports, and afterwards saw detective officers firing towards him. The officers were on the ground beside the van, which was on the left side of the road between the car lines and the kerb. Witness was beckoned forward by one of the police officers, and he, with others, lifted the inspector into his own van, and motored him to the Infirmary, but by the time he arrived there the inspector seemed to be dead. Witness added that when he heard the shooting he hid under the dashboard of the car, and consequently was not able to identify anybody.

Cross-examined by Mr Sandeman, witness said that the only men he saw firing were the detectives, though shots were coming from the back of his van.

Constable Main spoke of seeing a man whom he identified as William Fullerton, running down High Street, holding something inside his jacket with one hand and grasping it from the outside of his jacket with the other hand.

James Fullerton and Mitchell were seen by Constable Brown turning into Duke Street and going down High Street.

Cross examined, this constable said he identified two other men who were in the neighbourhood of the attack, but who were not now among the accused. The names of these two men were not divulged. They will appear for the defence.

Detective-Sergeant George Stirton, who was wounded in the attack made on the prison van, and mentioned in reply to counsel that he had experience of revolver firing in the Army, and had won the D.C.M., said he was present with Superintendent's Keith and Noble on 28th April, when a man named Frank Carty or Somers was arrested in the house of the accused O'Hagan. Proceeding to describe what happened on May 4, he said he was instructed by Superintendent Keith to accompany Inspector Johnston and Detective Macdonald on the patrol van, which was to convey Carty from the police office to Duke Street Prison. Two of the escort were armed. Carty was placed in the front compartment and another prisoner was in the rear compartment, accompanied by two constables. The van door was locked from the outside. Constable Ross drove the patrol van, Macdonald was next to him, witness was next, and Johnston sat on witness's left. They left the Central Police Office about 12.15. and arrived in the neighbourhood of the prison about 12.20. Nothing untoward had happened till then. When about ten or 15 yards from the Drygate, witness heard a shot, and he saw three men coming from the direction of the prison wall in the Drygate into High Street. They lined up on the pavement and fired shots at the motor patrol van. Witness immediately fired through the windscreen of the van in the direction of the men, and called out to his brother officers, "There you are!"

Witness was just in the act of firing at one of the three men he had noticed first when he was shot in the arm, and his revolver dropped. He did not fire a second shot. Witness stopped to pick up his revolver with his left hand, and said to Johnston, "You take this, I am hit." It was not until then he discovered there was something seriously wrong with Johnston. After that he heard firing in the rear of the car, and on looking round he saw five or seven men in the back of the van. They came from the direction of the close at the south wall of Duke Street Prison. There was also a line of men across the street at the corner of Rotten Row. They were firing revolvers. He attempted to fire in the direction of the men at the Rotten Row side. At that minute something seemed to go wrong, as they broke up and retreated, firing as they went. Immediately that happened the men in the rear of the van also went back. He saw them firing revolvers. Witness was in the Royal Infirmary till 4th June and was told he had been pretty ill for a time.

On Thursday, 26th, he was taken from the Royal Infirmary to Duke Street Prison, and shown over twenty men. He was able to identify nine of them – Mitchell, Grier, McCarra, McGarrigle, Carney, William Fullerton, O'Carroll, O'Daire, and Kavanagh. Mitchell was one of the men witness saw at the back of the van, about six or eight feet away, and he also saw William Fullerton there. Grier and O'Daire were in the group of men firing revolvers in the High Street on the Rotten Row side. Witness saw O'Daire replace a revolver in his pocket. He could not recall the exact position of Kavanagh and O'Carroll, but recognised their features quite well. McCarra was one of the first men he saw taking part in the attack. McGarrigle was on the same side of High Street, but witness could not say whether he was one of the first three men he observed.

By Mr Sandeman – You have identified nine people and you had two minutes in which to see them. Have you got a special capacity for identifying people? Witness –It is a thing I take credit for. People I identify I identify without a doubt. If there were any doubts I should accept it.

Did you think it was any good firing through a glass screen? Witness – Yes. Did you think you would hit anything? – I don't know.

Referring to witness's description of elbow shooting, Mr Sandeman observed, "Are you not attempting to make the jury think that three people were marksmen?"

In reply to Mr Mackay, witness said that it was the first time he had known armed officers to convey prisoners to Duke Street Prison.

Mr Mackay – Was not your shot the first of a series? Witness – That is not the case. I retaliated. I did not open the offensive. My instruction is that when a police officer is armed his revolver is only to be used when attacked and shot at.

Mr Mackay used the phase, "overcome by fear," to which witness replied, "I don't think the Glasgow police are so frightened as to be overcome by fear."

Then the hearing was adjourned until Wednesday.

Detective-Sergeant Stirton appeared in the witness box for continued cross-examination when the trial was resumed in Edinburgh High Court on Wednesday. Stirton stated that he had identified nine of the accused on two occasions as men who had taken part in the armed attack on the prison van. He identified them by their general appearance and their features and he did not know their names. He had no doubt about the men he had identified.

The witness simply pointed them out in court and did not give their names.

Detective-Constable Murdoch Macdonald, of the Central Division, Glasgow Police, was the next witness examined. MacDonald was described as a dark-visaged young man – a voice with the soft, pronounced accent which they acquire in the Western Isles.

"Here They Come"

Detective Macdonald told that he was seated next to the driver. When the driver was changing gears at the site of the attack, three men appeared and Stirton rose and exclaimed – "Here they come."

The leader of the attackers fired and the others fired after him. The witness was armed and fired at them through the windscreen.

When the men began to retreat, the witness ran round to the back of the van and saw two men working at the door. They ran away. Both were armed.

The witness identified six of the accused a few days after the attack. These were O'Carroll, Grier, McCarra, Campbell, William Fullerton and O'Daire.

Mr Sandeman – Can you tell me how McCarra was dressed? – No.

Did Johnston receive his wound immediately after the firing began? – I can't say. The first shot was fired from Rottenrow side, and the general firing began at once, as if the first shot had been a signal.

Did you see whether O'Carroll actually fired or not? – The men all had revolvers in their hands and were shooting.

Do you think it is a very sensible thing to fire through a screen? – Yes. In some circumstances it is necessary to get in very quickly when one is attacked.

A Question Pressed

A sharp passage between counsel and the witness was produced by one of Mr Sandeman's next questions. It was – Did you shortly before this case, state to anyone that you were not really able to clearly identify anyone?

Mr Macdonald – Lots of people ask for information in the detective department and they must take what answers they get.

That's all very nice, Macdonald, said Mr Sandeman, but when I ask a question I keep on saying it until I get an answer. This question will be read to you, and you will answer it without hedging.

The question was read by the official shorthand writer, and witness said, "I couldn't be sure of the second man, who ran down in front of me although I thought it was Mitchell."

Mr Sandeman – You are trying to get away again. You understand the question quite well; and if you refuse to answer – Lord Scott-Dickson – he is not refusing to answer.

Mr Sandeman after further pressing, sat down without having received a more definite answer to his question.

Cross-examined by Mr Aitchison, the witness admitted he had said something outside different to which he said inside the court regarding identification, but commented that unauthorised people who tried to pump him could take what they got. He had told people who had no right to question him what they wanted to know.

Counsel asked witness if he had not made a statement that he could only identify one man. – This is utterly wrong rejoined the witness.

I want to put this to you – Do you admit having as regards this matter of identification, said something outside the court different to what you have said here today?

Witness – Yes. If people try to pump information out of you they can take what they get. People ask for information who have no right to the information.
I suppose you recognise that agents for the accused have a right to ask for information? – Yes, but not one of them precognosced me.

After some wrangling with his catechist, witness repeated – I admit to telling unauthorised people, people who had no right to ask the question, what they were wanting to know. That was, I put them off. (laughter)

Will you answer the question, sir? – What did you tell the unauthorised persons? – If you tell me the unauthorised persons you mean I may be able to tell you.

What did you tell them? – I told them what it suited me to tell them.

After much wrestling of this description witness said the persons he had spoken to outside included several constables of the Central Division. He did not say the same thing to them at all. One of the constables he said, had asked him how they were getting on with the case, and he told him as much as it suited him.

"We were specially warned," added witness, "not to give anything away. We had got well warned by the detectives not to tell anything."
Mr Aitchison – Have you at anytime said – "I have no hesitation in identifying X quite definitely as one of these men, but I will not be able to definitely identify any of the other men there present"? – No, I did not say that.

To no one? – No.
At any time? – No.

Mr Aitchison asked which of Macdonald's statements was able to be taken as the truth, and witness answered that he was giving the true statement that day, adding – "I am on oath now."

Mr Aitchison – And it is only on oath you tell the truth?

Thomas Ross, the driver of the van, explained that when the firing started he ducked and his foot slipped off the accelerator with the result that the van stopped.

He identified among the accused Mitchell, Grier, McCarra, McGarrigle, Campbell, William Fullerton, O'Carroll and O'Daire and Kavanagh.

Witness's mention of Kavanagh's name caused something of a stir, and the Lord Justice-Clerk pointed out that Kavanagh had not been named previously by witness.

The Solicitor-General – He has not been named up to date.

Witness – All with the exception of Kavanagh. I did not see him fire.

The Lord Justice-Clerk – We are dealing with the eight men you identified on May 6. Never mind Kavanagh at present.

Mr Sandeman - Did you know any of the accused before May 4? – No, sir.
Had you seen any of them before? No, sir.

How does it come that you are able to name all those you identify here? – When I was identifying them at the police office an officer noted the names as I pointed out the men.

And all the time since then you have remembered the names and are able to read them off today. How far were the men from you? About 12 or 15 yards.

Mr Mackay – Weren't you trying to take cover yourself? – Yes.

Continuing his cross-examination, Mr Mackay asked – Were you taken round the cells at the Central Police Office before you identified the men on May 6? – No, sir.

Next day in the gymnasium hall, when a number of men were paraded before you, did you again fail to identify O'Daire? – That is not true, sir.

Mr Aitchison – Would you agree that the whole affair was over in about two minutes? – About that.

And during that time you saw these nine men who you identify sufficiently well to recognise them again? – Yes.

That gives about 15 seconds to each man, does it not? – That is so. And these men were entire strangers to you? – Yes.

Ad you pretend that you can identify nine men with absolute confidence under such circumstances? – I don't pretend; I'm sure of it.

Can you tell me if any police records in any country contain the record of any such a feat of identification? – When you see a large number of men with revolvers aiming at a vehicle and its occupants, of whom you are one, I think it would impress their features on your memory.

By Mr Sandeman – The first shot was some distance off, and too far off, witness thought, for it to have been fired from the van.

Constable David Brown, who was inside the van, said he heard about 20 or 30 shots. He instructed the prisoner who was with him to lie down and he himself stooped. During the attack he heard the door being shaken.

The Solicitor-General then announced to the jury that that concluded the evidence of the police officials on the van and also the evidence of the attack. He proposed next to ask the jury to follow him while he endeavoured to show the events which followed the attack on the motor, beginning with the visit of police officials to 74 Abercromby Street.

Detective Lachlan Macdonald, of the Southern Division, said that, accompanied by other officers, he visited the tenement there on the evening of the day of the outrage. They thought it right to go into every house on the stair. When they came out of a house on the first landing they heard the footsteps of a man coming from the top flat, and when they reached the second landing they met a man who gave his name as Rev. Father MacRory, of St Mary's Chapel House, which witness interpolated was almost opposite 74 Abercromby Street.

After their interview with Father MacRory the police went into a house on the top flat occupied by a Mrs Mulholland, which was on the opposite side of the landing from that occupied by the Campbell's. They came out of Mulholland's house shortly afterwards and saw the accused Grier go forward to the door of Campbell's house and knock. Grier said he was a traveller in fountain pens, and was looking for a man named Campbell. The police searched him, and found eight letters, but no documents to vouch for his identity. By this time the door of Campbell's house was opened by a young lady named Jane Campbell. They asked her if she knew Grier, and she replied, "No." Witness went into the house and met Vincent Campbell, one of the accused coming out of the parlour. The other officers followed, and took Grier with them. In the parlour were the prisoners Mitchell, McCarra and McGarrigle sitting on chairs. Vincent Campbell said he did not know Grier. Witness and his companions told the men that they were police officers making investigations into the outrage on the police van. They asked the men who they were. Mitchell replied that there was no racing on then, but that they were bookmakers in Ireland. At that stage other police officers arrived, and a search of the house was carried out, and a number of documents were found. One was the letter already read in Court calling a meeting of P.U.R. Committee, and signed Grier.

The lieutenant was examined at considerable length regarding the entries in a loose notebook which was found behind the piano. Papers found in the notebook showed collections of arms and explosives collected from Dumbarton, Motherwell, Blantyre, Edinburgh, Falkirk, Bannockburn, and Glasgow, West Calder, Winchburgh, Paisley, and Cambuslang, and also a note of a large quantity of these things despatched to Glasgow.

Witness stated that O'Hagan was arrested on the evening of May 4. He was charged then with harbouring the man Somers or Carty.

The Solicitor-General — What did he say he say in reply to the charge? — He replied — "I admit I had no right to do it. There is no person in Glasgow tonight more sorry than I am for the death of the inspector." O'Hagan admitted being a member of Sinn Fein.

By his Lordship – There was nothing said about the death of Inspector Johnston prior to O'Hagan's mention of it.

Dealing with the second visit made by the police about one o'clock in the morning to the house of Vincent Campbell, in Abercromby Street, witness stated that the note asking for 25 men to be on duty at Rottenrow was found under the mat in the parlour. Witness was asked to compare the paper on which the note was written with the leaves of the notebook, and stated that in size and ruling and in water mark the loose leaf corresponded exactly with those of the book.

The court adjourned at 4 o'clock.

When the prison van passed from the court in High Street a cheer was raised by a section of the spectators.

Thursday's Evidence

The proceedings were opened on Thursday morning with evidence by Sergeant Hugh McLeod, bar sergeant at the Central Police Office, who described the search at the police office of the prisoners arrested at 74 Abercromby Street, and a number of documents containing some mysterious entries which were found. Mitchell had no papers of importance and £8 9s in money, but in the possession of Grier was found a notebook containing written matter. Inside the front cover was a number of addresses, among them 89 Barlogan Avenue, the address at which Carney resided. Grier had £4 9s 5 ½ d in money. On McGarrigle's person was found what appeared to be a leaf from a notebook, on which the following was written: – "To John McG., – I want to see you tonight. – Dunne."

The Solicitor-General – Look at the notebook again. Among the list of addresses do you find an entry, 69 Absf. P.? – Yes.

The Lord Justice-Clerk – What is that?

The Solicitor-General – The suggestion of the Crown is that that represents 69 Abbotsford Place, the house occupied by the accused O'Hagan, in which the man Carty was found. McGarrigle also had a sum of £3 10s odds in cash, said the witness.

90

In reply to further questions by the Solicitor-General, he found a notebook (produced) on the accused McCarra. On the first page were written the following entries: – "Wednesday, 30th March, 1921, received £1; Thursday March 31 '21 received 10s; Thursday March 31, to Edinburgh and local expenses, 10s; Saturday, 2nd April, '21, received £1; Tuesday 5th April, '21, local expenses 5s."

The next line on the page read: – "J Docherty, 101 Roseberry Street, Lochee, Dundee." On the last page of the notebook there was an address, J. Cochrane (Hagan) 69 Abbotsford Place. There was a sum of £1 2s in McCarra's possession. With regard to the accused Vincent Campbell, witness said he found upon him a book bearing to be issued by Dan Harrigan, commission agent, 33 Hope Street, Glasgow. It contained betting rules and racing information, and there were a number of blank leaves for notes. On one of the blank leaves he found the entry – "Go to Forsyth, gas works, Firhill, early tomorrow." Another entry read – "To W.C., Derry, 800 dts. (which witness took to mean detonators), 20 ditto, six autos (which he considered meant automatic pistols), 6.25 amm. (ammunition). Please invoice above to H.Q. (headquarters)." The initials " D.D." followed.

Witness was next examined regarding documents which had been found in the possession of Vincent Campbell. He identified three leaves as those which had been taken from the pocket of Campbell. One there was the words, "Forsyth, Glass works," written in pencil. On another there were the words, "Please give bearer two casks as arranged. Enclosed fifteen shillings." To that the signature "Dunne" was appended. There was in the possession of the prisoner Campbell when searched the sum of £9 13s 3d.

In cross-examination by Mr Mackay, witness said there was nothing suspicious about the possession of such sums of money as were found on the prisoners.

Mr Aitchison cross-examined witness as to the method adopted in the police office of marking documents and other articles found on prisoners. Witness said they were labelled.

Why did you not label them in this case? – The detective officers did that.

Is it not unusual for the officer taking the documents to label them? – He signs them.

Why did you not sign them in this case? – I did sign them.

May I take it that you, although you were present and took the documents from the prisoners, did not mark them yourself? – I have not labelled them myself but I signed the labels.

Counsel – I am speaking at the moment of the four documents said to have been found on Vincent Campbell. Witness – I did not mark them.

As regards the labels, isn't that done at a later stage? – As soon as possible.

It may be a considerable time? – A couple of hours.

Was it Derry?

The reason I put this to you is this – Yesterday Detective-Lieut. Lachlan Macdonald, in answer to a question by me, said he searched Vincent Campbell in the house at 74 Abercromby Street, prior to his arrest and found nothing on him. I put it to you that you are in error when you say that these documents were found on Vincent Campbell? – They were found on Vincent Campbell.

Mr Aitchison then handed to witness the note beginning, "The bearer will arrange with you re buying the stuff, "remarking that on the second sheet witness had read McWhinny, 33 Westland Avenue, 'Derry. Just look at it again, he said, and tell me where you find 'Derry? – Witness again read the address, concluding with 'Derry.

Mr Aitchison read it, letter by letter. Does it not read D-r-e-n-y – it might be taken for that.

But your evidence is that it is 'Derry? – Yes.

Mr Russell next cross-examined witness on behalf of McGarrigle, asking if on that prisoner anything else was found in addition to what he had spoken of. Did you for example, find four war medals? Mr Aitchison asked witness to look at several productions for the

92

defence which, witness said, were a Military Medal, The 1914-15 Star, A General Service Medal, and the Victory Medal. Were these asked counsel, found on McGarrigle? – Yes. Did you ask McGarrigle how he got it? – No.

Mr Duffes - In the list of addresses which includes A.B.S.F.P., isn't there an alternative address to that, namely, 181 West Scotland Street? – Yes.

Do you know if O'Hagan has anything to do with 181 West Scotland Street? – I could not say.

Opposite some of these entries do you find entries dealing with drapery goods? – Yes.

Which seems to indicate that the person who had that book was interested in canvassing for orders? – Quite so.

In re-examination by the Solicitor-General, witness stated that the initials A.W. which appeared on the separate documents or covering sheets were those of Superintendent Auchterlonie Williamson.

The leaves found in Campbell's possession were handed to the jury to be examined and compared with the leaves of the notebook. One of the counsel for the defence complained that the prosecution was suggesting that the leaves were actually taken from the book; an assumption, which he declared, was quite unsupported by any evidence. He did not dispute that the leaves were similar to those in the notebook.

His Lordship put the point to the jury, remarking that so far as the evidence had gone there was nothing to show that these were taken from this particular book. The position of the defence was that there were thousands of these books and millions of these leaves.

Professor Glaister, Glasgow, gave evidence regarding the post mortem examination of Johnston's body. The bullet had entered the breast, and penetrated the heart and other organs.

Alexander Drysdale, Governor of Duke Street Prison, said he was responsible for the censoring of correspondence of any untried prisoners detained. All the accused were warned that letters must be plain and intelligible.

On May 12 the head warder brought him a letter which Mitchell had written. In the witness's opinion it was not one he could permit to go out of prison. He told Mitchell that the letter did not conform to the rules, and that there must be no ambiguity in the language of the letter.

The witness retained the original letter which he handed to the police.

Mr Mackay for the defence took objection to this letter being produced in evidence against any of the accused. He held that the Governor should have returned the letter to the accused; otherwise a trap was laid for accused persons, which was contrary to our ideas of the administration of justice.

After further discussion, Lord Scott-Dickson said he would give his judgement next day on the question raised, which he said, was going to be a vital matter.

During the course of the trial Mr Mackay informed his Lordship that he was told that some of the police who had given evidence had been in conversation with witnesses who had not yet given evidence.

His Lordship said that the Crown would take steps to ensure that the witness who had given evidence would not converse with those that had still to be examined.

At a later stage the Solicitor-General denied that there was any ground for the complaint.

The Lord Justice-Clerk gave his ruling in the dispute on Friday, and Crown counsel then led further circumstantial evidence in support of the suggestion which had been canvassed by the prosecution since the beginning of the trial that Mitchell had been one of the leaders of

Sinn Fein in Scotland, and therefore, apparently, worthy of the attention of the law.

Lord Scott-Dickson's ruling on the contention was that, having regard to the limited purpose for which the Solicitor-General proposed to use the letter, namely only for the purpose of comparison of handwriting, he could not exclude it as proof of the case.

Mr Drysdale, Governor of Duke Street Prison, said the letter was signed by James Mitchell and was addressed to a man in Foley Street, Dublin.

The Identifications

Cross-questioned by Mr Aitichison for the defence, witness said he would accept with hesitation the evidence of two policemen who claimed to identify eight and nine men who were strangers to them, and whom they had seen for only two minutes. Asked regarding the type of men who were paraded at Duke Street Prison for identification witness said they were all of the same class – Sinn Feiners or Irishmen.

His Lordship – Is there any speciality about the features of a Sinn Feiner or Irishman? (laughter)

Two Manchester warders, John D. Whitehead and Thomas H. Wareing, identified Mitchell as Daniel Patrick Walsh, who had escaped from Strangeways Prison, Manchester, on October 25, 1919.[1]

A Glasgow constable identified Grier as a spirit salesman named Daniel Branniff.

Evidence was given regarding the arrest of Kavanagh in a house at 734 Dobbie's Loan. When charged at the police office in connection with the murder of Inspector Johnston, Kavanagh replied, "I refuse to say anything."

A Caledonian railway official said that Kavanagh was an employee. The official record showed that he was working on May 2 and 3, but not on May 4, and that he was working on May 5 and 6.

95

Inspector F. T. Barker, of the Auxiliary Division RIC was next in the box.

A series of debates arose concerning the right on the part of the prosecution to produce and read certain letters found in Dublin.

Witness said that he searched a house in Dublin occupied by Michael Collins, Finance Minister to the Irish Republic, and found there a document addressed to Mr Dan Branniff, Glasgow.

Objection was raised to the evidence, and it was decided to exclude the reading of the letter.

Witness searched another house in Dublin, which was occupied by John Dunne, Brigadier Quartermaster of the IRA. He was familiar with Dunne's handwriting.

Witness was shown a loose leaf pocket book found at Campbell's house in Abercromby Street, Glasgow, in which were certain pages where Dunne's name appeared. He was of the opinion that the handwriting in the book was very similar to that of Dunne.

On the court resuming, the cross-examination of Inspector Barker was continued.
Re-examined by Mr Aitchison, witness said he had no warrant to search the office of Michael Collins and that no warrant was required.

Archibald Norman Glover of the RIC, Dublin, was examined by the Solicitor-General, and he said he was with the previous witness on 4th April at the search of the office of Michael Collins in Dublin.
The witnesses recognised the documents produced as having been found on that occasion.

After further evidence regarding the documents in the case and the police inquiries, John Brown, 13 Bath Street, Glasgow, handwriting expert, gave evidence as to the handwriting of several of the accused, particularly with regard to Mitchell and Grier, found on the documents produced.

In cross-examination the witness said that in his opinion none of the handwriting that he had had examined was disguised.

It was, however, unusual for anyone to sign his name with different spellings, as was shown in the case of Dunne.

Dr Moira E N McAlpine, MB, ChB, Glasgow Royal Infirmary, who attended to Stirton's wounds, in answer to Mr Sandeman, KC, said she considered that Stirton had been seriously injured to the danger of his life, in respect that if blood poisoning had set in it might easily have proved fatal. Stirton suffered seriously from loss of blood.

By Mr Aitchison – When admitted to the Infirmary Stirton was faint and spoke with a shaky voice. He had all his senses, but she could not say whether he was afterwards a bit confused in his recollection of what had happened. In the case of a patient who had lost a good deal of blood the memory might be unreliable immediately afterwards, but later on the memory revived and could recall events as they happened at the time.

By Mr Russell – During his convalescence Stirton was visited by his police friends, but said she did not know whether he discussed with them the events that had happened.

Dr James H Pringle, MB, CM, FRCS, Glasgow, corroborated.

O'Hagan's Breakdown

On Monday morning, for the first time since the trial began, the prisoners were not placed at the bar on the stroke of the hour for starting business.

When the prisoners entered the dock it was noticed that O'Hagan, one of the older men, was missing from his usual seat in the back row.

At the start the Solicitor-General (Mr D C Murray KC), referred to O'Hagan's absence and explained that it had been reported to the Crown authorities yesterday that on Saturday night this prisoner had become unwell, apparently suffering from some mental disorder. The information was given last night at a medical examination with a view to ascertaining his condition and the doctors who had examined O'Hagan would give the result of that examination.

Dr Harvie, the medical officer of Calton Prison, said he had examined O'Hagan yesterday morning, and formed the opinion that he was insane. His medical condition was such that he was not in a position to give further instructions for his defence in this trial, and that he could not, without prejudice, be brought to the Court.

Similar evidence was given by two medical practitioners who examined O'Hagan that morning.

The Solicitor-General intimated that in view of this evidence he would move that the diet against O'Hagan be deserted simpliciter.

Mr Duffes then said he thought it was right on behalf of Mr O'Hagan and his relatives to intimate that he did not accept the Crown action here as an act of grace, but an act of justice, even less than justice. He had only been waiting an opportunity of raising a question which would have met with the same result.

He proposed to draw the Solicitor-General's attention to the fact that there was no evidence upon which he would have been entitled to ask for a verdict from the jury against his client. In fact, at the close of the Crown case he would have asked the Solicitor-General if he felt justified in asking for a verdict against O'Hagan.

The Lord Justice Clerk said he entirely agreed with what the Crown proposed to do and with a great deal of what Mr Duffes had said. There seemed to have been a very weak case against O'Hagan, if there was a case at all.

He advised the jury to return a formal verdict of not guilty against O'Hagan, the result of which would be given him in charge of his friends who were present.

The jury unanimously adopted the direction of his Lordship.

O'Hagan is about 45 years of age and carries on business as a confectioner at Abbotsford Place, where he resided. He is also understood to be interested in several business concerns in the city. It was in O'Hagan's house that the Glasgow police arrested Carty.

The Crown then closed their case by calling Detective-Lieutenant John Forbes, Eastern Division, who gave evidence as to the discovery after examination in a store of at the extreme back court at 74 Abercromby Street, of firearms and ammunition.

My Mr Mackay – There were no doors in the close at 74 Abercromby Street, and a rope only fastened the door of the shed.

Case for Defence

Mr Sandeman KC, in opening the case for the defence, asked that one of the Crown witnesses who had not been examined by the Solicitor-General should be called. It was stated by Crown counsel that up till yesterday they had been unsuccessfully searching for that person.

Mr Sandeman called as the first witness for the defence Mrs Tracey, wife of Thomas Tracey, one of the prisoners. Witness said her husband carried on business as an undertaker at Westmuir Street. She helped him in his business. The police arrested her and her husband on the evening of May 4, and she had been kept in prison for eleven weeks and two days. The witness showed some emotion at the recollection of this experience.

Mr Sandeman asked her what is the first incident of that day you remember? – A young man came in about eight o'clock and ordered a taxi cab to be sent to the Ivanhoe Hotel in Buchanan Street. She did not know the man.

Are you connected with Sinn Fein or the Irish Republican Army? – No.

And so far as you know had your husband been engaged in the Sinn Fein or Irish Republican Army movement? – No, so far as I know.

Did you know anything of the men in front of you, pointing to the prisoners in the dock? – No, I don't know any of them.

Witness, continuing her evidence, that at the time she got the order for a taxi her husband was in bed. He got up that morning after the children had gone to school. That was at half past nine to a quarter to ten. Her husband was making arrangements for the funeral that day of a young man named Gordon who had been killed by being run over by a charabanc. In the forenoon her husband went along to the Gordon's house at 753 Shettleston Road to make final arrangements for the funeral which was to take place at three thirty in the afternoon. He left shortly after eleven accompanied by a man named Brennan, who sometimes helped him in his business. Her husband returned between 12.30 and 1. He afterwards had his lunch and left after it to go to the funeral. Witness added that she saw no signs whatever of any agitation on the part of her husband that day. It was quite an ordinary business day for them until the evening.

James Brennan, steel smelter, stated that he had known Tracey for seven years or more, and sometimes gave him a hand with his work. He went to help him on May 4. He arrived about a quarter to ten o'clock and waited for Tracey in the shop. Tracey and he then looked at the newspaper, discussed the news, and then started work. Witness afterwards went down with Tracey to the Gordon's house at Shettleston in connection with the funeral of the lad Gordon, who was killed by a motorcar. They got to the Gordon's house about half past eleven.

After Tracey visited the house, they passed the time till the opening of the public houses, but then determined to go to Parkhead, as the beer was better. (laughter) About ten minutes past twelve they had a drink in a public house. Witness left Tracey about 25 minutes past twelve near his house.

Cross-examined by the Solicitor-General, witness said there was nothing that drew his attention specifically to the time that morning, except the opening of the public house. (laughter)

James Gordon, the next witness, said he had a brother killed by a motorcar on April 30, and it was arranged that the funeral should take place on May 4. Witness left his sister's house at 20 minutes past twelve in the forenoon, and when he got to the end of the road he met Tracey and Brennan. It was 20 minutes past eleven when he left his sister's house, and it would take ten minutes to walk to where he met Tracey and his assistant.

David Stirling, in reply to Mr Sandeman, said he had known Tracey a good many years. He remembered that on the forenoon of May 4 he saw Mr Tracey. Witness was standing in Main Street, Shettleston.

This was between 11.30 and 12 o'clock. He was certain about that. Tracey was with Brennan, and they were going eastwards.

Peter Gordon, another brother of the late Andrew Gordon, gave evidence of Tracey's visit to the house. The time, he said, was about a quarter or ten minutes to twelve o'clock.

William Craig, a hairdresser, said Tracey was a customer in the shop in which he worked, and Tracey came into the shop on May 4 about half past twelve, and witness was practising a song for a competition which was to be held in St Andrew's Hall, and knowing from conversations with him that Tracey was interested in music he sang it over to him. That fixed the circumstances of the visit in his mind. Tracey left the shop about a quarter to one.

Alexander Gordon corroborated the evidence of his brothers, and Mrs Cairns, an old lady who resided at 15 James Street, Shettleston, stated that she saw Mr Tracey at his shop about half past twelve as she was passing. He was standing at the shop looking at a newspaper.

The Case for O'Carroll

Mr Sandeman stated that he had several witnesses to corroborate further, but he was not to call them. He would proceed now with the case of O'Carroll.

Mrs O'Carroll, mother of the accused Michael O'Carroll, was the next witness.

Replying to Mr Sandeman, witness said her son was a member of the Thomas Ashe Sinn Fein Club, and she was a member too. She did not know any of the other prisoners as friends of Michael's. On May 4 Michael was in bed until 12 o'clock. There were present her husband, their daughters Maggie and Bridget, and a boarder named John O'Carroll. They had dinner together. It would be about one or five past one o'clock when dinner was finished. Michael's first outing was to the Labour Bureau. She remembered a man, McLachlan, coming to see her son regarding a suit being fitted on. That was about half past eleven. He found Michael in bed. A man Troy, a ship's painter, came to the house for a boot repairing last about 20 or 25 minutes past 12.

Margaret O'Carroll, 7 Hope Street, Anderston, a young lady, smartly attired, stated that her brother was in bed when she left for work at about eight o'clock on May 4, and that when she returned for dinner about 25 minutes past twelve o'clock her brother came into the room with his coat off as if just out of bed.

Mr O'Carroll, father of Michael O'Carroll, John O'Carroll, labourer, J McLachlan, tailor, and John Troy, ship's painter, corroborated.

The Case for Carney

John McKenna, an apprentice barber, employed by Carney, stated that Carney on May 4 came to business at twelve o'clock. He was later than usual.

Cross-examined, witness said that Mrs Carney came to her husband's shop usually with his dinner. On this particular day Mrs Carney arrived at the shop five or ten minutes earlier than her husband.

Michael Connolly, with whom O'Daire lived, spoke to O'Daire being in his house at Possilpark on May 4 at 11.40. His wife told him that O'Daire left the house about noon.

A girl of 16 spoke to meeting O'Daire in Possilpark shortly after 12 noon.

Mrs Connolly stated that O'Daire came to her home in Possilpark on May 4th at 12.15 and left about 1.30 with her son Louis.

Louis Carroll, 18 years, 88 Mansion Street, stated that he was an intimate friend of O'Daire. He remembered May 4. On that day, when he came home for dinner about one o'clock, he found O'Daire there. O'Daire was an apprentice engineer with John Brown and Co., Clydebank. After taking dinner witness left the house with O'Daire. They proceeded to the house of John McGuire, 792 Hawthorn Street, Springburn. They stayed there for some time, and witness afterwards accompanied O'Daire to Turner Street, where the latter went into the house of the Fullertons for the loan of a bicycle.

James McGuire corroborated.

Sean O'Daire then entered the witness box and gave an account of his movements on the morning of May 4. Mr Mackay then proceeded to cross-examine the witness as to the identifications at the Central Police Court and Duke Street.

After a lengthy examination, evidence was led in support of the alibi of the accused Mitchell.

Mrs Mary Lavin, 173 Thomson Street, Glasgow, stated that Mitchell lodged with her for about two months. He had a key for the door. On the evening of 3rd May witness did not hear Mitchell come home, but she knew he occupied his room. She found in the morning that he had eaten his supper, and she knocked him up about ten o'clock.

Mr Mackay – It is suggested that this man Mitchell was in the Ivanhoe Hotel on the Sunday and Monday nights. Do you know if that is so? – No. He did not sleep out any of these nights.

After she had knocked him up on that morning of May 4, witness proceeded; Mitchell came into the kitchen and left the house again about a quarter past twelve. She was sure of the day, because her house was twice searched that night.

Patrick Lavin, her husband, told a similar story.

Mr Ryan, Superintendent of the Irish National Insurance Company, gave evidence of being in Mitchell's company in the early part of the day.

Francis Milroy and Bernard Callan of the same Company corroborated Miss Frances Smith and William James Fullerton spoke of Mitchell's movements.

An expert in handwriting, Mr Woodland, Edinburgh, stated in examination that while there were similarities between the writing in Mitchell's letter which was impounded by the Governor of Duke Street Prison and the writing on a number of the documentary productions, including that over the signature of Dunne, there were also dissimilarities which suggested that the handwriting was by different persons.

He dealt with difference in the formation of certain letters.

Grier's defence was then opened. His landlady and her assistant said that he left his lodgings at 12 noon on May 4 with a parcel of underclothing and returned at 2.30pm.

Mrs McCallum, 100 Main Street, Bridgeton, told that on May 4, Grier came to her house with shirts and handkerchiefs to wash. She had been doing washing for him. He arrived about 12.25.

Mr McCall, organising secretary of the Shop Assistant's Union, told that he saw Grier about a quarter to one on May 4 sitting on a west going car in Gallowgate. They waved hands to each other.

Francis Mallon, 63 Auchentoshan Terrace, Springburn, spoke on behalf of James Fullerton. Mallon said that Fullerton came to his house at 12 o'clock on 4th May, and did not leave until a quarter past one, when he went out with witness. A sister corroborated his evidence.

Evidence on behalf of James McCarra was then led. Mrs McGovern, 60 Glasgow Road, Cambuslang, said McCarra was in the house on 4th May up till the time when she went out her messages at a quarter past eleven, and when she returned at one McCarra was away. He came in at three o'clock for dinner.

Edward Docherty, miner, spoke to himself and McCarra having a drink in a public house at Hamilton at the time of the attack. Corroborative evidence was led.

Mrs Fullerton and Miss Mary Fullerton stated William was in the house at 12.15.

Kavanagh's case was taken next. Elizabeth Abercromby said she spoke to him in Phoenix Park on the 4th May at about one o'clock.

Mrs Smith and Mrs McTaggart, Dobbie's Loan, gave evidence that they had seen Kavanagh from 11.30 or 12 noon till about twenty minutes to one on the 4th May.

James Kavanagh went into the witness box. Detailing his movements of that day, he said he was in St Aloysius Chapel in the morning. He was not in High Street at the time of the shooting. After leaving the chapel, he then went on to Dobbie's Loan. He stayed there for an hour, and left at twenty minutes to one to go to Phoenix Park.

Miss Donoghue, newsagent, Abercromby Street, testified McGarrigle called at her shop at 12 noon on 4th May.

Mr Downie stated that McGarrigle was in an office at Hope Street at 12.15.

George Buchart, 96 Oran Street, Glasgow, on 4th May remembered calling at Mr Harrigan's office for his parcels about 20 minutes past 12. There were two persons there, William Downie and John McGarrigle.

The accused John McGarrigle then went into the witness box and gave a lucid account of his movements during the day.

Mr Russell, at the conclusion of McGarrigle's examination, intimated that he had reached the end of his case, and Mr Condie Sandeman also stated that the Crown having failed to produce a certain witness whom he desired to examine he formally closed his case.

This closed the evidence, and at eleven o'clock on Thursday the Solicitor-General rose to address the jury on behalf of the Crown. It was not only their right but their duty to weigh carefully all the items of evidence and disseminate as to the character of that evidence in relation to the accused.

There was a great mass of documents, part of which only had been able to put before them, but before he was done he would ask for patience while he tried if he could to piece together the information and the evidence derived from the documents.

Counsel directed the attention of the jury first to the conspiracy charge, and took up the case of Walsh or Mitchell. Comparatively little was known of Mitchell, he said, until his arrival in Glasgow about the beginning of March when he turned up at the office of the Socialist and Research Bureau and without being asked any questions and as a total stranger was taken home by the witness Lavin. Mitchell was not his real name, but an alias. That was proved by the evidence of the two prison warders, who had had him in their custody under the name of Daniel Patrick Walsh. As to Mitchell being also the same man as Dunne, they had the evidence of the handwriting expert who had no hesitation in saying that in certain letters Mitchell's was identical in writing to those on documents signed Dunne. The evidence was quite clear to the effect that Dunne was not engaged in any other than an illegal conspiracy to obtain arms.

A Traveller in Pens

Proceeding to deal with Branniff or Grier, he said that he represented himself on arrest as a traveller in fountain pens, but he looked as if he had to? His name was not Charles Grier but Daniel Branniff, and he was the man to whom the letter was addressed that was found in Michael Collins house in Dublin.

Daniel Branniff, Scottish representative on the Supreme Council of the IRB, 1918-1921.

The Solicitor-General then viewed the evidence led before the jury for the case of each of the accused and dealt with the documents and the references about the collection of firearms and ammunition relating to them individually and the association which existed between some of them which supported the charges.

106

So far as Tracey was concerned, the Solicitor-General stated he had nothing in the way of documents apart from the mysterious appearance in Tracey's possession of a precognition or statement by Miss Lee in regard to the Alloa case.

In regard to Kavanagh, was the undoubted fact that he was connected with Sinn Fein, and had in his possession the keys of the Sinn Fein headquarters.

The weight of evidence was very heavy upon the conspiracy that centred round the illegal trafficking in arms, and was especially so with regard to the five men who were arrested in No.74 Abercromby Street - namely Mitchell, Grier, McCarra, Campbell and McGarrigle. So far as the last named was concerned, there is not the same weight of evidence against him.

With regard to the two Fullertons, Tracey, O'Carroll and Kavanagh, he would not be fully justified in asking for a verdict on documentary evidence alone. Carney was amply involved, but as for O'Daire there was only the matter of the bullet.

His Lordship – I don't think three cartridges would matter anyway. Of course that was for the jury.

Counsel then proceeded to deal with the second charge – the conspiracy which ended in the disaster of 4th May, and which involved the murder of Inspector Johnston and the wounding of Detective Stirton. There was a curious similarity between the tour of the taxi cab on the night before and the tour on the morning of the 4th May.

Notes

1. The rescue of six Republican prisoners in broad daylight from Strangeways Prison was one of the most daring IRA prison escapes in the War of Independence.
    During the early months of 1919, a number of Republican prisoners serving sentences ranging from six months to two years were sent to Strangeways Prison. The 13 prisoners under the command of Austin Stack immediately began to plan an escape.

Stack decided to use the method by which 20 Republican prisoners had successfully escaped from Mountjoy Prison in March 1919 by scaling the wall with a rope ladder thrown over from the outside. The plan was approved by IRA GHQ Staff in Dublin and Rory O'Connor and Peadar Clancy were sent over to England to organise the breakout.

The prisoners soon established communication with O'Connor and elaborate details of the overall plans were conveyed to him by prisoners upon their release. Communications from the outside were sent in by visitors and by messages concealed in food parcels.

By late September only six Republican prisoners remained in Strangeways. Each evening before lock-up between 5pm and 5.30pm, the prisoners were allowed out to exercise in a small yard that was enclosed by a ring of high railings. Outside the railings stood a wall some 40 feet high.

When the appointed time for the escape came the six prisoners – D.P. Walsh, Stack, Beaslai, Paddy McCarthy, Con Connolly and Seán Doran overpowered a warder and made their way to the outer wall and signalled to their comrades outside to throw over the rope. After some difficulty the prisoners eventually climbed to the top of the wall and down the patent ladder on the outside.

In addition to O'Connor and Clancy, who were in charge of the rescue, more than 20 Volunteers mostly immigrant Irish, took part in the operation outside the jail and, in broad daylight, held up everyone who attempted to pass along the street.

The six escapees were taken to 'safe' houses in Manchester and after several days were smuggled from Liverpool to Dublin on the B&I steamer. One year later Seán Doran was recaptured and sent back to Strangeways. McCarthy was shot dead by the Black and Tans and D.P. Walsh was arrested in Scotland. All the others evaded capture.

Chapter 6

Verdict

The following report of the conclusion of the trial appeared in the 27th August edition of the *Glasgow Observer*. Again, this chapter continues as a verbatim account taken directly.

ALL ACCUSED ACQUITTED: A FACER FOR GLASGOW POLICE

Lord Scott-Dickson Criticises Identification Procedure

What has become popularly known as the "prison van case" was concluded on Saturday in Edinburgh High Court with the acquittal of all the accused.

The charges against the accused had fallen flat. There may be some satisfaction to certain people in the knowledge that nearly all the detained young men, who were in regular employment, have lost their situations. But very much worse is the plight of the Glasgow police after the outspoken criticism by Lord Scott-Dickson.

NO REDRESS

Apparently the law allows no question of compensation. Not even in the case of those who were not tried, yet were imprisoned for eleven weeks, as with the treatment meted out to Rev. Father MacRory of St Mary's, and seventeen others.

The police have, undoubtedly, as the counsel for the accused pointed out in his final address, been suffering from what in vulgar parlance is termed "wind up." But this wholesale arresting and forceful imprisonment of people, including a blameless clergyman, does not lead to amicable feelings among the Irish people. However it is enough that all are free.

Lord Scott-Dickson, before whom the case was held, began his charge to the jury at five minutes past ten o'clock on Saturday by reviewing the evidence on the charge of conspiracy and dealing with the documents produced. He pointed out that as far as the charge of conspiracy for the purpose of furthering the objectives of Sinn Fein or other organisations by the unlawful use of force and violence was concerned, this was practically independent of what took place at Cathedral Square, and a man might be involved in conspiracy under the first charge and yet have nothing to do with the shooting at Cathedral Square.

The first charge was much less serious than the second, because the second charge, in either of its alternatives, was one of murder. If there was conviction there would be no alternative for him but to pronounce sentence of death.

THE DOCUMENTS

His Lordship was to comment upon the association of prisoners with the documents. He pointed out that Tracey was practically not involved, and that there was no documentary evidence whatever against O'Daire. As to the police discovery of three bullets in the camera case in O'Daire's lodging, O'Daire explained that he got the bullets from a brother when he was in Ireland, and he pointed out that the bullets were not in a case, but in a complete camera, with the operating portion of it confined to a small space at one end. The police did not understand the camera, and thought it was merely a case. The fact that the camera was demobilised, so to speak, when produced in court was nothing against O'Daire, and nothing against the camera. It had been badly used when brought there. That was all there was; nothing in that in his view.

The Solicitor-General had said that on the documentary evidence he would not be justified in asking for a conviction on the first charge as to either of the Fullertons, Tracey, O'Carroll, or Kavanagh. The only document, which was associated with McGarrigle, was the note left on his mantelpiece – "I would like to see you tomorrow, J Dunne," and so far as his Lordship could judge he could not say that made any case at all against McGarrigle as far as the first charge was concerned. So he added McGarrigle to those names. The result was that would leave five men behind, excluding the two Fullertons, Tracey, O'Carroll, Kavanagh, O'Daire, and McGarrigle. Apart from the documentary evidence, was there any evidence except what he had referred to that undoubtedly there was an organisation in Scotland, particularly in Glasgow, which was engaging itself in collecting arms all over the country in order that they might be sent to Ireland. Where were they found? A great lot of the documents, if they

110

believed the police, were found in 74 Abercromby Street or in Carney's possession, and a few of them in Dublin.

A FLAW

Were they satisfied that the detectives were right when they said where and on whom they found these documents? They followed the usual practice so far as the criminal authorities were concerned. The defence was that the police did not initial them at the time or write on the documents at the time where they were found. That was true. It was no answer for the Crown to say they followed the system. If the jury thought they could not rely, so far as the finding of the documents at the particular place or on the particular man was concerned, they would still have the documents, undoubtedly found at some of the places which the police searched, and it would be for them to say whether those documents did not show that one or all of the five men – he excluded seven – were actually concerned in an organisation existing in Scotland which made it their job to get firearms and explosives in Scotland, to collect them to Edinburgh and Glasgow, and to despatch them to Ireland. The documents, to his mind, seemed to show there were such an organisation and such a business being carried on.

IDENTIFICATION

Referring to the identification of the accused, his Lordship said it had been suggested that the police, in dealing with the identification, were deliberately marking out men so that witnesses who would not have identified them otherwise would identify them.

That would be a most dastardly thing to do. Talk of crime! There could not be a worse crime than for members of the police by chicanery of that kind to get an identification.

It was a tremendously serious charge, a most offensive charge, and it would be for the jury to consider that.

Passing on to deal with the second part of the charge, the Lord Justice-Clerk said he had the greatest possible difficulty in dealing with it; there was such a mass of evidence. He proposed only to make some general observations. In the first place, they took the Crown case alone; leaving out of account the trouble about identification, there was ample evidence, he thought, against all twelve men of having been at Cathedral Square at the time of the shooting.

THE TRAGEDY

Mr Sandeman intervened with a remark about Tracey, and his Lordship then pointed out that the proof against Tracey, if there was any proof, was that he was at the scene in the morning before the shooting took place at all. Coming to the attack, he said it was clear that the men who were there with arms were there of set purpose by arrangement with the view of getting Carty out of the van. They did not want to kill Johnston or wound Stirton. What they wanted was to smash the van and get Carty out. It was for the jury to say, having regard to the evidence, whether they had any doubt that some people had arranged to make an attempt to rescue Carty on the way to the prison. It was very probable that the men who were preparing this attack did not expect the police to be armed. It was very rare in this country for the police to be armed and in point of fact they were told that the two officers were armed only because the police got word from Ireland that there was to be an attempt at rescue. It was quite true that none of these young men who went to rescue Carty dreamt they were going to come in for murder or commit murder, but there was no doubt Johnston was just as clearly murdered as if they had met him on the street and pulled out a revolver and shot him through the heart. It was murder, and nothing else, and it did not make it less murder in the eye of the law that the original intention was not to murder Johnston but to get Carty out of the van. It was a gross crime to try and take a man by force out of the hands of the police, and if in the doing of an illegal thing firearms were used and some of the police who were doing their duty were killed, that was plain murder and nothing else. The law was that if they conspired to do an illegal thing and used firearms in the course of doing it, and carried the intention into execution to the extent of going up to the police where the van was and firing at it and hitting two of the men sitting in front and killing one of them and wounding the officer, this was murder.

THE ALIBIS

Lord Scott-Dickson said an alibi was sometimes regarded as a doubtful defence, but it was a perfectly good defence if it was

112

established to their satisfaction. Each of the prisoners had stated an alibi which they submitted was sufficient to show that whoever did the shooting at Cathedral Square they could not have been concerned in it because they were somewhere else.

It covered only a very short space of time, because the actual shooting took two or three minutes. The men dispersed certainly before the half hour. The time Crown said several of them were there as early as 10 o'clock, and if they did not remain all the time till 12.30, they were at any rate there from 12 till the attack failed. It was a pure question of fact, and it was for them to say.

The jury retired at 1.35. They asked to be supplied with all the documents to which the Lord Justice-Clerk had referred in his summing up.

The jury returned after an absence of over an hour and a half, re-entering the court at 3.13.

THE VERDICT

Councillor Archibald, foreman of the jury, announced the verdict as follows:-

Daniel Patrick Walsh alias Joseph Dunne (1) not proven; (2) not proven
Daniel Branniff alias Charles Grier (1) not proven; (2) not proven.
James McCarra (1) not proven; (2) not proven.
John McGarrigle (1) not proven; (2) not proven.
Vincent Campbell (1) not proven; (2) not proven.
John Carney (1) not proven; (2) not proven.
William Fullerton (1) not proven; (2) not proven.
Michael O'Carroll (1) not proven; (2) not proven.
Sean O'Daire (1) not proven; (2) not proven.
James Kavanagh (1) not proven; (2) not proven.
Thomas Tracey (1) not proven; (2) not proven.
James Fullerton (1) not proven; (2) not proven.

The numbers relate to the charge – (1) being that of conspiracy and (2) that of murder.

All the accused were accordingly acquitted.

113

Mitchell or Walsh was immediately re-arrested however. It will be recalled that in the evidence against him he had escaped from Strangeways Prison in Manchester. He was one of the party that disappeared with Austin Stack.

BACK TO FREEDOM

Parliament Square was kept comparatively clear of the public during the sitting, but a large crowd collected in the High Street to hear the verdict, and the news created unbounded delight to a considerable section of it, many people waving miniature green flags.

Vincent Campbell (centre) receiving congratulations.

Several members of the jury were treated to a special ovation, while the released eleven were mobbed and cheered and attempts made to carry them shoulder high down the High Street.

Group of released men and their friends outside the Court.

SCENES IN GLASGOW

News of the acquittal soon spread in Glasgow, and a large number of friends gathered at Queen Street Station to meet the 5pm train from Waverley in which the liberated men travelled.

Commandant John Carney (centre) with his wife and a friend.

115

Abercromby Street was once more gay with bunting and the dear tricolour and scenes reminiscent of the release of Father MacRory were witnessed.

Hundreds of flags were flown from windows of the houses in the main streets of the Calton district, while great crowds assembled in Abercromby Street.

At 8pm there was a general movement to St Mary's Church, and for a couple of hours thereafter an unbroken procession of parishioners entered and left the church, taking a few minutes to utter prayers of thanksgiving.

Thomas Tracey had a rousing reception on returning home to Parkhead. He was carried shoulder high by enthusiastic friends who escorted him in triumph to his house, from the window of which he addressed the crowd.

A special reception was organised by the Alderman Thomas McCurtain Sinn Fein Club in the League Hall for their released friends. According to the *Glasgow Observer* "The scene in Henrietta Street baffles description – it surpassed even the reception accorded to Father MacRory. The League Hall, the Boys Guild and the various other rooms were crowded to the door, and it was with the greatest difficulty that the released prisoners could enter the Hall. The Rev. Dr McEwan introduced the 'prisoners' in both Halls, and Mr Daniel Branniff responded in Irish first and then in English, advising prudence on the part of all his bearers. They were grateful, indeed, to be among their friends again, and his only regret was the absence of their gentlemanly and admired Commandant, whom they hoped to welcome soon on his release."

Commenting on the acquittals the *Glasgow Observer* noted that even the *Glasgow Herald* acknowledged that the acquittal of the men "cannot have come as a surprise to anyone who followed the evidence with attention."

"In our view the released men owed their acquittal mainly to the ability of their counsel in shattering the credibility of some of the Crown witnesses and to over eagerness of some of those witnesses to prove too much."

The judge too displayed a judicial dispassion which cannot have failed to influence the jury's decision. Lord Scott-Dickson was a Tory MP before his appointment to the Bench, but he seems to have acquired the British tradition of judicial impartiality which the judicial bench in Ireland so sadly lack.

Of course, the accused men were innocent. Their alibis were convincingly proved.

A CONTRAST

The results of the trial bring into sharp contrast the administration of British law in Britain as compared with Ireland. Had the innocent men accused and now acquitted appeared before any British tribunal in Ireland, police evidence would have been adopted unhesitatingly and conviction would have followed. That is why in Britain it rests on the confidence of the public and is upheld by that.

At Manchester on Tuesday D.P. Walsh was charged with escaping from Strangeways Jail in October 1919. Walsh protested his detention, stating that it was a breach of the truce between England and Ireland. Under the truce, he contended, warrants for the arrest of members of the Irish Army were suspended. He demanded to be put in communication with the Home Secretary, and that his leaders in Dublin should be informed of the breach of the truce. He was remanded until Thursday. Walsh was on Thursday discharged, the British Home Secretary having advised the police to offer no evidence against him.

The last, however, had not been heard of the "prison van case," for three men arrested on 18th July had still to be put on trial. They were Frederick Quinn, Éamonn Mooney and his brother Seaghan.

In the 22nd October 1921 edition of the *Glasgow Observer*, it was announced that:

> "Frederick Quinn, Eamonn Mooney, Sean Mooney and Charles Ferguson, who were arrested in connection with the shooting of Inspector Johnston have been liberated, the charge against them being withdrawn. This was attributed to the strong stance taken by Sinn Fein in Scotland. Just after the arrest of the first three men Mr O'Sheehan, the Sinn Fein

117

Organiser, proceeded to Dublin and represented to the Chief Liaison Officer there, that this was a breach of the truce. Negotiations were set on foot between Dublin Castle and London in regard to the matter but no definite decision was come to. A suggestion from a certain quarter that the truce did not apply to Scotland was met by the retort that such a view would cut two ways. On the recent arrest of Charles Ferguson, the Standing Committee of Sinn Fein in Scotland sent a strong letter of protest to the Irish Delegates, against this further breach of the truce, and Mr O'Sheehan again proceeding to Dublin followed this up. The matter was immediately taken up direct with Downing Street, and the release of the imprisoned men is the result. The *Glasgow Observer* opined that, "It is a matter for satisfaction that they have got out without further trouble, but it is a matter for regret that the British officials in Scotland had to be forced into this ungracious manner of repairing their breach of the truce."

Having provided the account of the trial and the verdicts in the Glasgow Prison Van Case as reported in the *Glasgow Observer* the next chapter will piece together the inside story of the attempt to rescue Brigadier Frank Carty from the prison van.

Chapter 7

Inside Story of the Ambush

This chapter will describe both the official rescue plan that emanated from GHQ in Dublin and also the attack on the prison van that was actually enacted on 4th May 1921.

The account of the rescue attempt is drawn mainly from some of the participants. I am indebted to Cathleen Knowles McGuirk for a handwritten statement by her late uncle Seaghan Mooney, who describes his own part in the ambush. I have also used the recollections of the rescue bid as related to the journalist John Cooney by Michael O'Carroll, who also took part in the episode. It is contained in *The Irish Republican Brotherhood in Scotland: The Untold Stories of Andrew Fagan and Michael O'Carroll*, and is edited from three hours of tape recorded reminiscences and interviews, plus notes.[1] In addition I refer to written statements made to the Bureau of Military History by Frank Carty, the object of the rescue bid, and Joseph Booker and Patrick Mills who at the time both served in the Scottish Brigade of the IRA.[2]

The official plan to free Carty is described in the autobiography of Charles J McGuinness, *Nomad*.[3] It is also retold in *Liam Mellows and the Irish Revolution*.[4]

The Official Plan

Charles McGuinness, the man who rescued Carty from Derry Jail once again enters the story. One day, while resting in the Donegal hills, a dispatch bearer approached one of the sentries. He carried a dispatch for McGuinness from the O.C. of the IRA in Derry enclosing another from Dublin. The letter stated that Frank Carty, the Sligo commandant, had been arrested in Glasgow, and would be sent back to Derry, under heavy guard, for execution. The name of the steamer was given, and the probable date of the sailing. Under this factual statement was a terse message written in Gaelic as follows:

'I want you to investigate this problem, and if there is any way of effecting a rescue, I want you to try and am confident of your ability to succeed.

'Regards

(signed) MICHAEL COLLINS[5]

Collins who was Director of Intelligence of the IRA signed the dispatch with a nom de plume known only to Republican commanders.

Michael Collins, Director of Intelligence.

Accompanied by six men armed with automatics and carrying twenty rounds of ammunition each, McGuinness set out for Glasgow aboard one of his colliers the *Carricklee*. He conceived a plan involving nothing less than piracy on the high seas. They planned to return on the boat with Carty and attempt a rescue at sea. McGuinness was confident he could get Carty over the side into a small craft. He knew that the steward of the ship and several members of the crew, being sympathetic to the Republican cause, could be depended upon to assist.

McGuinness recollects the episode in his book 'Nomad':

> "Dressed as labourers and carrying red bandannas to secrete our guns, we submitted ourselves to the scrutiny of the guards at the gangway, and then took up our steerage quarters. The steward and friendly members of the crew, when called into our confidence, swore to help our plans to capture the vessel on its return with Carty. We carried sufficient medical dope to paralyse the whole British Army, and the steward agreed to brew a pot of tea for the sentries on the return trip at an appointed time, heavily charged with the anaesthetic. Then, when they had succumbed to the drug, we would take the keys and unlock the strong room in which Carty would be held prisoner. At this stage we would ascend the bridge, hold up the skipper and his officers, and stop the ship when abreast Inishowen Head (on the Derry-Donegal border)."

The Glasgow IRA were notified of the plan in a letter from the Officer in Command of the Derry Brigade dated 3 April, which read: "We have a plan whereby Frank C. may be taken from the escort on board the steamer to Derry. A lot depends on the assistance you can arrange on your side".[6] The letter was personally delivered by George Armstrong, an Intelligence Officer in the Derry Brigade. He worked on the 'Scotch boat' and was the courier between Dublin, Derry and Glasgow.[7] But the plan was doomed even as it was made.

The Unofficial Plan

When McGuinness (who was using the alias Hennessey) and his comrades arrived in Glasgow, they proceeded to the Sinn Féin headquarters at 171 Renfield Street, to find the place a beehive of industry.[8] The premises were jammed with men busily overhauling Colt 45's, Webleys, Smith and Wessons and other less modern weaponry. McGuinness takes up the story, "Promptly I gave my credentials to the commanding officer, and stated the purpose of my mission. He frowned and shook his head. 'Sorry Hennessy, but we have decided to stage the rescue right here in Glasgow. We'll stick up the prison van in an hour's time. I have every hope of success.' 'If I call off our attack', went on the Commander, 'it would shatter the whole Republican movement here. Anyway, I doubt if they'd obey me, so our original scheme will have to prevail.' 'Perhaps you're right', I agreed. 'But I'm afraid you'll never get Frank Carty out of a prison van in broad daylight - in the heart of Glasgow."[9]

McGuinness was not the only Republican to hold this opinion. Liam Mellows, Quartermaster General of the IRA, was made aware of the local plan whilst in Glasgow to investigate the Scottish accounts.[10] He attended a meeting at Elliot's public house, the 'Bunch of Grapes', at Paisley Road Toll.[11] There he found the local men discussing a desperate adventure, which was no less than a repetition of the Manchester Rescue of 1867.

Liam Mellows.

Mellows cautioned against this in favour of the official plan, and argued that it would be foolish to jeopardise the flow of arms by rousing a public outcry in Scotland. But the plans were already in motion for the rescue bid to be enacted the following day. Anticipating the wave of arrests that followed, Mellows wisely left Glasgow at once.[12] Joseph Booker recalls that a meeting was held in the evening of the 3rd of May in Abercromby Street opposite St Mary's Church (probably in Vincent Campbell's house at no. 74) at the request of Commandant D.P. Walsh at which arrangements were made to attack the prison van the following day. Booker noted that among those present at the meeting were Father MacRory, the young curate who was a chaplain in the First Battalion of the Scottish Brigade, John Carney, a barber from Govan and Commanding Officer of the Scottish Brigade, and Seán Flood from Dublin who was a Brigade Adjutant. At the meeting D.P. Walsh addressed the logistical problem of which of several vans that would be leaving the Central District Court would convey Frank Carty to the prison. Walsh arranged that Cumann na mBan member Annie Murray, would cycle ahead of Carty's van. She was to be tipped off by an old woman, who was a cleaner in the Central Police Station. Walsh gave this woman a description of Carty. Her instruction was to throw out her bucket and mop, as Carty's van was about to leave. This would be the signal for Annie Murray to start peddling up the hill and alert the Volunteers who would be waiting in readiness to ambush the van and free their comrade.[13]

The former Central Police Court which now houses the Glasgow Police Museum.

The IRA volunteers that were selected to take part in the rescue attempt were all members of a flying column or active service unit, and were chiefly used for operations in the west of Scotland and occasionally as far east as Leith and Edinburgh. They were recruited from various companies in the First Battalion area and consisted of between twenty and thirty men.[14]

At this meeting Michael O'Carroll and Joseph Booker were instructed to mobilise the men in the active service unit to take part in the rescue attempt and detail them where to assemble the following morning. The two men visited houses in Maryhill and Springburn and the surrounding areas. "The landladies in most cases were very indignant and demanded to know why we wanted the men at this time of night." Both men were also tasked with visiting the dumps to lift the required arms to supply the attacking party, and Booker who did not take part in the ambush, recalls having to obtain a sledge-hammer to be used to force the door of the prison van open. In addition they had to spend time arranging alibis for the men and that kept them busy well into the next morning.[15] Booker recalls delivering six automatic weapons on the morning of the attack to his commander, D.P. Walsh at the Ivanhoe Hotel in Buchanan Street.

Seaghan Mooney, who as we shall see played an active role in the rescue attempt, gives the following detailed account of the ambush.

> "On the stroke of midnight, May 3rd, my mother called me as a result of a number of imperative knocks at the door. She told me that Michael O'Carroll was in the kitchen, and was anxious to see me, so I told her to bring him into the bedroom. When he ushered me in he wasted no time in cognising me of his mission, as he told me himself, he had a lot of calling to do before morning. He instructed me to get my brother Éamonn and mobilise six men of our Company (B of the First) and order them to be at the Tollbooth at ten o'clock, fully armed, and await further instructions from the Commandant, who would be present at the appointed hour.
>
> To mobilise six men would not appear to be a difficult task, but most of the men were migratory workers and moved around a good deal. Unlike the men at home they never sought a transfer as they had a certain *(word unclear)* for B Company. This made our job rather arduous to say the least.

124

Our potential volunteers were to be located in districts as far apart as Parkhead, Anderston, Bridgeton and the Gorbals. We were in Maryhill. However, we started on our mission at 1 a.m. in the morning of the fourth, and after a lot of furtive dodging of police patrols, whom we did not wish to alarm, we managed to mobilise the six men. Some of them were in lodgings, and shared the same room with other members of our Company, and our ingenuity was taxed to the utmost trying to mollify the men who were not being mobilised. An amusing incident occurred when we were mobilising the Sergeant, 'needler' Doyle...When we finally located the apartment the walls were so thin that we could hear the occupants of the rooms actually snoring. When we knocked at Doyle's door we got no reply so we gave a double reminder of a more imperative nature to our sleeping beauty. He awoke suddenly, and in a hoarse voice asked 'who is it?' My brother replied Éamonn, 'Jesus, Mary and Joseph' he ejaculated, 'G Men'.[16] For the next five minutes we could hear him hustling around probably burning incriminating documents. When the men were finally 'mobbed' we repaired for home. I think it was nearly seven o'clock.

We boarded a tram at 9.30 a.m. to meet the men at the appointed rendezvous. In those days most of the trams had an open vestibule front and rear. We proceeded to the upper deck of the vehicle and passed along to the front opening, which was divorced from the main portion by a sliding door. There were three people already seated on the limited horseshoe seat, and, to our surprise we recognised them as an officer and two other members of A Company. It was impossible to sit with them and maintain a rigid silence, as our friendship was mutual. To our great relief we discovered after a few introductory remarks that their interest in the weather was every bit as keen as ours. When we had exhausted all the vagaries of the atmosphere phenomena we still had a few stops to go. I was on the verge of saying this is where we get off when their leader J Fullerton, suddenly stood up and said that this was their destination. I sighed with relief.

When we got to the Tollbooth we noticed some men from B Company hanging around, and we approached them. We were hardly five minutes together when we were accosted by our three fellow travellers, who had also been mobilised. I suppressed an inward chuckle on seeing them once more, but I also felt an inward pride at knowing that although we all espoused the one cause, we never talked about a 'job' to each other until we were positive that the other person was actually engaged on the same mission.

At ten o'clock we received orders to form into smaller groups and designate one man from each to meet at a certain café in London Street where we would receive fuller instructions about what was to take place. Five of our men were left, I think, in Hanover Street, and Captain Quinn, my brother and I repaired to the café. We received further orders from the Commandant about the intended engagement, and he told us in detail what it was.

One of our men who was in charge of a flying column had been arrested after breaking out of two jails. He was awaiting an escort to take him back to Derry Jail for trial. He was at present lodged in the judiciary and would appear in court that morning. This was just a matter of form, as most prisoners went through this formula. He would then be taken in the prison van to Duke Street Prison, and that's where we came in.

The men were to be divided into three groups, which would cooperate but not merge. The three parties consisted of a reconnoitring unit or outposts, a labour section and an attacking column (I was in the latter). He then explained to us to get in touch with our respective parties and get our men posted immediately. There were six men placed on outpost duty every hundred yards or so from the Court to within two hundred yards of the prison. The labour section kept together, without drawing attention unduly. One unit grouped for a few moments to receive our post positions. When the Captain had told us to go to our stations we broke up casually.

Adjutant Seaghan Mooney.

My instructions were to go to the far side of the street, facing the prison wall. When I surveyed the situation I found that I was isolated, being the only armed man on the *(word unclear)* side of the vehicle. On the gaol side were at least four men, and further up at the turn of the wall were two others. I thought this a grave error of judgement for on thinking of the engagement in an anticipatory manner I realised that not only would I be in great danger from my own men's fire, but, if they succeeded in forcing the occupants of the van out, I should not be able to cope with them myself. As it so transpired this contretemps almost happened.

At 12.35 midday I was watching one of the labour unit crossing the street with a three-foot parcel, under his arm, what looked suspiciously like a crow bar (I later learned when he went into action that it was a sledge hammer), when I noticed our Sergeant signalling. A few minutes later the van loomed into sight.

The psychological moment having arrived I tensed myself inwardly, but to the passer by I was only a young man casually leaning against a lamp standard. I placed my hand in my pocket, and crooked the trigger of my Smith and Wesson .45. When the vehicle was ten yards away I noticed four men in the driver's cabin. They seemed to be alert and tense, as though expecting something to happen. They were not disappointed. When the car drew abreast of me I stepped off the path, and hesitated, to give the occupants the impression that I only wished to cross the street. In another instant I sprang on the running board and grabbed the windscreen. When I ordered them to stop the van they didn't seem to hear, the reason being that one of the men in front stepped out to the middle of the road, stooped on one knee and pointed his gun at the police. As he was twenty or thirty yards away the guardians of the law thought that they had a good chance of foiling a hold up so two of them drew guns and commenced to fire. At this point their attention was drawn by the men on the offside who had their guns levelled at the interior of the cabin. I began to realise my unfortunate position for if they were forced to fire, I was just as liable to be on the receiving end as the hapless quartet on the driver's seat. While all this was flashing through my mind I began to act fast. I focused my attention on the nearest man, who was Inspector Johnston and told him to get out. He obliged all right but not of his own volition. He toppled across my left arm, knocking me on the street, and dove head first on to the cobblestones, an inert mass. While I was gazing at him the next man, Detective Sergeant Stirton clattered down the step and was about to fire when I winged him in the arm. He made a grab for his gun, which fell from his grasp at the momentarily paralysing effect of the bullet, but as it was near my feet I kicked it underneath the prison van.

When I took stock of the situation I began to feel more confident that we had it well in hand, for I could keep these two men under control (I wasn't aware that the Inspector was dead) the rest of the boys should be able to contend with the rest. However, all things were not equal.

A SECOND GROUP FIRED AT THE DOOR OF THE VAN

INSPECTOR KILLED DETECTIVE WOUNDED

ONE GROUP FIRED FROM IN FRONT OF PRISON VAN

A newspaper composite of the rescue attempt (inset, Inspector Johnston).

Constable Macdonald and the other men were still blazing away, and to make matters worse the car was beginning to roll backwards down the steep hill. Our gallant squad had not succeeded in making much of an impression on the steel door of the vehicle, and they had begun to fire into the lock. Everything was going against us just when victory seemed to be in sight. I was also thinking of a raid a few weeks previously when I had the foresight to bring with me a crow-bar, and the apparent ease with which the bar sprung the door open. However, it was no use thinking of this now. Suddenly my Captain signalled to me from the far side. I

129

mistook the signal for 'take cover' so I went back towards the path and put a lamp post between danger and me. After a couple of minutes I realised that the column were withdrawing, and as the Captain was still signalling at me to get back, I knew that he meant me to retire. With a quick glance around to ensure that none of my men required help, I retired up Rotten Row."

The following account of the ambush by Michael O'Carroll is similar to that of Mooney's with both men claiming responsibility for injuring Detective Sergeant Stirton.

"As the van came up and changed gear - it was the old gauge change - the position I had was right at the rear of the van, about thirty feet from where the van had stopped to change gear. It was then that Seán Adair (called O'Daire in the trial) and Éamonn Mooney came out to hold up the van. Stirton fired through the windscreen. The minute he did there was a reply and Johnston fell mortally wounded out of the side. I saw him lying there. Stirton ran round to the front of the van across on the far side. I took cover behind one of the standards. I saw him coming. I took a random shot. I got him in the arm and the gun fell from his hand. He lifted it and ran back under a hail."[17]

Cooney then relates what O'Carroll went on to tell him.

"While the men in the front attacked the escort with the driver, another party attempted to smash open the rear door. John Coyne, who was a hefty man, was given a sledgehammer. If there was any difficulty in extracting the keys from whoever was in possession of them, his job was to smash the lock of the door. But after some minutes of strenuous effort, he failed to smash the lock of the door. In increasing panic, one of the attackers fired at the lock but it would still not budge.[18]

O'Carroll continued: "Ross the driver, fair play to him, he crushed himself down and threw his machine into gear and drove away up the street at a slow pace. We had to be careful in the cross–fire not to get the man we were looking for shot in the van. The van wheeled right to the gates of

Duke Street, which were opened in a flash, and the van went right in."[19]

Frank Carty who heard the strenuous effort to release him, recalls that "after being taken from the van I was severely beaten by the police".[20]

O'Carroll describes the aftermath of the attack.

"What was I to do? I had a Webley in which one shot had been fired and, incidentally, it was the same calibre as Johnston was killed with. I was wearing an overcoat and a cap. I put the gun in my pocket. The van was gone. A man was lying dead. There was no contact from the top of the rear. I was the only one at the rear. I just calmly walked down the street, stood at the green tram stop and got on the tram. I went to Bridgeton to the house of my friend Maisie Mullins. She happened to be washing out the close at the time. I asked her if anybody was around. She said no. So I broke the revolver and threw the cartridges and the revolver into the bucket and said to her 'You know how to get rid of this when it is convenient'. She never asked any questions but she would have heard about the incident later.

I was not working at the time. I was signing on the buroo. So I thought quickly. When I got to the Labour Exchange it was about 12.45. I signed the register. That came out in the evidence. I went to an Irish house, to Miss Cassidy's. I changed my overcoat, cap and a bit of my appearance. There was no such thing as people running about. I was played out. I had an early bed. But about twelve o'clock there was a knock at the door. The boys were at the door and I was arrested. I was taken to Central Police Station. D.P. Walsh, Father MacRory and John Carney had already been arrested. They had a fair nucleus of those who were involved in the incident."[21]

O'Carroll claims that the reason why the police concentrated on Abercromby Street was because, "there was a call from Dundee from the parochial house - some time around one o'clock on May 4. It was supposed that the speaker spoke in Irish and that whoever transmitted that – or whatever tap or system they had at the time –

131

the police followed up the call from Dundee to the presbytery in Abercromby Street. This led them to the arrests of Father MacRory and D. P. Walsh. The priest was Father John Fahy. He was Irish. The murder squad were after him. Father Fahy knew about the whole thing. He made the unfortunate phone call. He spoke in Irish. I would say that it was the result of the phone call that the police concentrated on Abercromby Street."[22]

O'Carroll makes a very interesting claim and one that the author has been unable to corroborate. Contemplating what would have happened in the event that the jury decided to return a guilty verdict on the defendants at the trial in Edinburgh, O'Carroll was confident that they would still have been freed. He told John Cooney that Michael Collins had sent 'The Squad' (also known more fancifully as the Twelve Apostles) over from Dublin and they were staying in the Calton district. This was an elite unit whose job, with Dáil Cabinet sanction, was the highly dangerous task of eliminating those whose knowledge would have nullified the work so far achieved, as happened to every previous freedom movement in Ireland. Part of its job was to try and rescue prisoners, as happened on May 14th 1921, when they unsuccessfully attempted to free the leader of the North Longford flying column Seán MacEoin, the Blacksmith of Ballinalee, from Mountjoy Jail using a captured armoured car.[23]

O'Carroll claimed: "We knew they were on the outside. We had the whole thing worked out."

A few spine-shivering moments were experienced by the prisoners. "Ellis the hangman, sized us up in Duke Street jail before we went for trial. We were told by one of the warders that this was the procedure. They took our height and various things like that. That was the atmosphere when we went to trial in Edinburgh."

John Ellis carried out the execution of the Irish patriot Roger Casement who was sentenced for treason as a result of his part in the Easter Rising. Of Casement Ellis made the following comments, "The impression will ever remain on my mind of the composure of his noble countenance, the smile of contentment and happiness, as he willingly helped my assistant…the steady martial tread of his six feet four inches and soldierly appearance adding to the solemn echo of his prompt and coherent answers to the Roman Catholic chaplain while marching to his untimely doom. Roger Casement appeared to me the bravest man it fell to my unhappy lot to execute".[24] Ellis was also responsible for hanging the 18 years old medical student Kevin Barry, in November 1920, for his part in an ambush in which three British soldiers were killed.[25]

Significantly O'Carroll asserts that of the twelve prisoners who were put on trial – Frank O'Hagan, having been released, broken in health – four had not participated in the ambush.[26]

As might be expected, headquarters in Dublin were far from happy about the Glasgow rescue attempt. According to Joseph Booker, "Collins, I was told was greatly annoyed with Walsh over the arrested Volunteers in the attempted rescue of Carty, who was in Glasgow without authority."[27] This is corroborated by Patrick Mills who states, "D.P. Walsh was recalled and reprimanded by Michael Collins for the loss of the arrested men and dislocation of the organisation, through the attempted rescue of a man who had no authority to be in Scotland."[28]

IRA members who were mobilised for active service to rescue Brigadier Frank Carty

Name	Rank	Company
Daniel Patrick Walsh	Commandant, Assistant Quartermaster General for Headquarters	
Michael Doyle	Sergeant	A of the First Battalion
Seán Adair	Volunteer	A of the First Battalion
Seámus Fullerton	O.C. First Battalion	A of the First Battalion
J Kirkpatrick	Volunteer	A of the First Battalion
Patrick Ferry	Volunteer	A of the First Battalion
Thomas Gavigan	Volunteer	A of the First Battalion
Frederick Quinn (ex British Army)	Captain later OC	B of the First Battalion
Éamonn Mooney	Captain later Commandant	B of the First Battalion
Seaghan Mooney	Adjutant later First Lieutenant	B of the First Battalion
Liam Fullerton	Volunteer	B of the First Battalion
Vincent Campbell	Volunteer	B of the First Battalion
Seán Coyne	Volunteer	B of the First Battalion
Stephen Fallon	Volunteer	B of the First Battalion
John Carney	OC and Brigade OC	C of the First Battalion
Seán Flood	Quartermaster and Assistant Brigade QM	C of the First Battalion
Matthew Tipping	Volunteer	C of the First Battalion
John O'Brien	Volunteer	C of the First Battalion
Liam Tobin	Volunteer	C of the First Battalion
Thomas Docherty	OC	G of the First Battalion
Patrick Ryan	Quartermaster	G of the First Battalion
Charles Ferguson (ex sergeant of a machine gun corps in the British Army)	Volunteer	G of the First Battalion
Thomas Fenton	Volunteer	G of the First Battalion
J. Williamson (may have participated)	Volunteer	G of the First Battalion
Thomas Hickey	Volunteer	G of the First Battalion
Andrew Fagan	Captain, Officer in Charge of Purchases and Transport, and Quartermaster of the Scottish Brigade	C of the 2nd Battalion

This information came from an inventory of names of members of the Scottish Brigade of the IRA in the Éamonn Mooney papers.

Notes

1. John Cooney, 'The Irish Republican Brotherhood in Scotland: The Untold Stories of Andrew Fagan and Michael O'Carroll', *Celebrating Columba: Irish Scottish Connections 597-1997*, TM Devine and JF McMillan (eds.), John Donald, Edinburgh, 1999, p.137-154.
2. Witness statements were collected by the Bureau of Military History. Launched in 1947 by Minister for Defence Oscar Traynor. The bureau amassed 1,744 statements from people who participated in the War of Independence, including a small number from men who served in the Scottish Brigade of the IRA. As the historian Ann Matthews has noted in her essay in *The Impact of the 1916 Rising* (Ed. Ruan O'Donnell), Irish Academic Press, Dublin, 2008, witness statements have strengths and weaknesses. There is an element of subjectivity and bad memory and differences of perspective in some events.
3. Charles John McGuinness, *Nomad*, Methuen, London, 1934.
4. Desmond Greaves, *Liam Mellows and the Irish Revolution*, Lawrence & Wishart, London, 1971.
5. McGuinness, op cit, p.137.
6. The letter was produced as evidence at the trial in the Glasgow Prison Van Case.
7. Cooney, op cit, p.147.
8. The recently demolished Scottish Television (STV) studios, later occupied the site of the Sinn Féin headquarters and premises of the James Connolly Club. The James Connolly Club was the oldest continually functioning branch in the entire Sinn Féin organisation and existed well into the 1950s.
9. McGuinness, op cit, p.138.
10. There was a discrepancy in the accounting of money allocated to purchase arms in Scotland which Michael Collins was unable to resolve. In his essay, *Michael Collins in Scotland*, Ó Catháin states, "there wasn't an actual hole in the Scottish account books, more a virtual hole, created by the necessity of disguising the multiple supply lines, protecting IRB channels and ironically but most importantly protecting civilian contractors".
11. The building that the Bunch of Grapes occupied is demolished and should not be confused with The Grapes pub near Paisley Road Toll.
12. Greaves, op cit, p.232.
13. Cooney, op cit, p147.
14. EMP/5/31 Statement by Seaghan Mooney in the Éamonn Mooney papers
15. BMH statement by witness, Joseph Booker, NAI, BMH papers, WS 776, p.3.

16. G-men, the name given to the G Division which was the detective branch of the Dublin Military Police. The IRA effectively wiped it out by 1920.
17. Cooney, op cit, p.148.
18. Cooney, op cit, p148
19. Cooney, op cit, p148
20. Statement of Military Activities of Frank Carty, 1935, Sligo County Library, p.18.
21. Cooney, op cit p.149.
22. Cooney, op cit, pp.149-150. Father Fahy was chaplain of the 4th Battalion of the Scottish Brigade. He was an outspoken critic of English rule in Ireland. There was a story of how a number of soldiers from the Black Watch, Irishmen by birth, came to St Andrew's Cathedral in Dundee for Mass. However, along with the Mass, Father Fahy gave them a severe lecture, telling them they should be ashamed of serving in the British imperial army, adding they should be patriotic Irishmen and go home to fight for Ireland. In the 1950s the Scottish Brigade Old IRA Association presented Father Fahy with a gold watch in recognition of his services to the Brigade. Bob Stewart, *Breaking the Fetters*, Lawrence & Wishart, London, 1967, p.152-153; Brian S Murphy, 'The Stone of Destiny: Father John Fahy (1894-1969), Lia Fail and Smallholder Radicalism in Modern Irish Society', *Radical Irish Priests 1660-1970*, Edited by Gerard Moran, Four Courts Press Ltd, Dublin, 1998, p.185-218.
23. Patrick J Twohig, *Green Tears for Hecuba: Ireland's fight For Freedom*, Tower Books, County Cork, 1984, p.419.
24. Alfred Noyles, *The Accusing Ghost or Justice for Casement*, Victor Gollancz Ltd, London, p.158.
25. The famous ballad *Kevin Barry* was written within days of his execution by an Irish exile in Glasgow whose name is unknown.
26. Cooney, op cit, p.151.
27. BMH statement by witness, Joseph Booker, NAI, BMH papers, WS 776, p.4.
28. BMH statement by witness, Patrick Mills, NAI, BMH papers, WS 777, p.6.

Chapter 8

What Became of Them?

With all those arrested for alleged involvement in the attack on the prison van now released, they shared the hopes of the Irish people at home and abroad that the Anglo-Irish Treaty would deliver an honourable peace settlement.

The negotiations between British and Irish representatives began in London at Downing Street on 11th October 1921. The Irish delegation was led by Arthur Griffith and included Michael Collins. The British invitation for talks did not mention the Dáil. They had proscribed Dáil Éireann as an "illegal national assembly of the Irish Republic". The five Irish delegates presented no credentials on behalf of an Irish Republic when they came to discuss a settlement. British Prime Minister Lloyd George always talked of negotiating with Sinn Féin just as with any other Irish political party, and never with elected representatives of an existing Irish Republic.

The British conditions from the start were inflexible. Ireland had to remain in the empire and 'Ulster' must not be coerced.

The Treaty allowed for a self-governing dominion of two countries only, within the British Empire. The new Irish Free State would be permitted its own, but limited army, autonomy in internal affairs and, in theory, control over its revenues. It would not be a republic. Members of the Free State parliament would have to take oaths to the British monarch. The monarch would appoint a governor-general to reside in Dublin. British forces would keep strategic harbours and no Irish navy would be permitted, for 'security reasons'. And there were other tangible restrictions.

Acceptance of the Treaty meant abandonment of the Irish Republic which the Easter Rising had proclaimed and which had been democratically and constitutionally ratified by Dáil Éireann in January 1919. Griffith and Collins never seriously pressed the issue of the Republic, and the absent de Valera was ambivalent about it.

Griffith conceded to Lloyd George that six counties in the north could opt out of a united Ireland. Lloyd George promised that there would be a boundary commission which would adjust the border "in accordance with the wishes of the inhabitants, so far as may be compatible with economic and geographic conditions". Michael Collins assumed such a commission would give all of Tyrone and Fermanagh, plus parts of Derry, Armagh and Down to the Free State. He put his faith in the British government.

The Treaty was signed in London by the British and Irish delegates on the night of 5-6 December 1921, after two months of talks and under Lloyd George's sudden threat of "immediate and terrible war" if the Treaty was not signed the same night.

The Treaty debate in Dáil Éireann was contentious. The leadership of both Sinn Féin and the Army was divided and the ensuing arguments became increasingly bitter and the once unified Republican Movement split asunder. According to Dorothy McArdle: "...for the most part those who opposed the Treaty could see no good in it, looking down on it from the height of the Republic not up from the depths of subjection; seeing it as degradation and sheer loss; while those who defended its terms distorted and magnified them representing them as giving more than they gave. They declared that...it safeguarded Ireland's neutrality, involved no danger of partition...that it was independence in all but name". [1]

After the signing of the Treaty an effort was made by the IRA in Glasgow to empty the arms dumps in and around the city and make use of the Christmas season by getting the stuff across to Ireland in parcels. Several messengers were instructed to bring their material to the League of the Cross Parochial Hall in Tollcross. Everything was going to plan until the 23rd December when the Hall was raided. The police discovered arms and ammunition being packed into cases. There were 15 rifles, a number of revolvers and bombs, 2000 detonators, 4000 rounds of ammunition and gelignite. Thirteen Volunteers were arrested. Eight persons were tried at the High Court of Edinburgh for attempted smuggling of explosives and firearms to Ireland and five were sentenced to imprisonment. They were held in Barlinnie Prison until 12th February 1922 when they were released under a general amnesty for IRA prisoners.

One of the captured men was John McPeak. He was later to join the Free State Army and was the gunner of the *Slieve na mBhan* armoured car in which Collins made the fateful journey at Béal na mBláth in County Cork on 22 August 1922. There was a suspicion that McPeak had a role in the death of Michael Collins since shortly afterwards he defected to the Republicans taking the armoured car with him.[2]

John McPeak

The arguments for and against the Treaty have been many and varied and even now, in the opening years of the twenty first century, people still hold entrenched views on the matter. Both sides believed they were acting in the best interests of Ireland and it must be remembered that the ruling class in England has been a past master of the tactic of divide and rule.

The debate continued into January 1922. When the vote was taken on January 7th the result was 64 in favour and 57 against. The British got what they wanted by exploiting already existing divisions.

The Treaty effectively implemented the British Government of Ireland Act, partitioning Ireland and subverting the All-Ireland Republic, all of which overturned the clearly expressed will of the people of Ireland as demonstrated in the 1918 election, the last such all Ireland election to date.

It created two states. In the Six Counties a Unionist-dominated state with power devolved to Stormont carved out of the province of Ulster, which was gerrymandered so as to guarantee a permanent Unionist majority. In the 26 Counties a Southern Parliament was imposed in place of the 32 County Dáil Éireann.

The institutions of the Republic were dismantled. Sinn Féin was divided. Those who stood by the constitution of Sinn Féin and in defence of the Republic held on to the name Sinn Féin, those who accepted the Treaty of Surrender, as Republicans termed it, later went on to organise as Cumann na Gaedhael.

The anti-Treaty section of the IRA established an Executive and set up HQ in the Four Courts in April. In June 1922, Michael Collins, with artillery given to him by the British, gave the order to fire on the Four Courts and so began one of the saddest periods in Irish history, during which many hopes and dreams were dashed and the national unity and resolve of the previous four years was destroyed.[3]

In the early stages, severe fighting took place, as the Republicans took over towns and barracks, but they were gradually driven from their fortified positions, and the war moved into a guerrilla phase of ambushes and reprisals. The total casualty list by May 1923, when arms were dumped, amounted to between 500 and 800 Free State troops killed and probably higher casualties among the Republicans, but there are no precise figures. It is clear, however, that casualties were considerably in excess of the number of Irish Volunteers lost in the 1916-21 period. The Civil War has been described as a counter-revolution with the powerful forces of the property owning classes and the Church by-and-large siding with the Free State. Liam Mellows, who was executed on 8 December 1922 on the orders of the Free State Cabinet, along with Rory O'Connor, Joe McKelvey and Dick Barrett, came to realise before it was too late that the Republic was lost unless it was able to mobilise the mass of workers and small farmers behind it.

The divisions in Ireland were mirrored in Scotland. Men and women who stood shoulder-to-shoulder during the 'four glorious years' were now on opposing sides. However, evidence shows that in Scotland the majority of the Movement stood by the Republic with only a small fraction responding to Michael Collins' order to the Scottish Brigade in June 1922 to join the Free State Army.

The respective protagonists in Ireland sent their representatives to tour Scotland and espouse their opposing positions. Countess Markievicz addressed 10 meetings in Glasgow on the Republican perspective, and also spoke to audiences in Clydebank, Alexandria, Craigneuk, Coatbridge, Dundee and Edinburgh. Within the Scottish Executive of Sinn Féin there was an anti-Treaty majority. In March 1922 de Valera and his followers founded Cumann Poblacht na hÉireann and consequently Republicans in Scotland dissolved Sinn Féin and founded Cumann Poblacht na hÉireann nAlbain which easily eclipsed its Free State rival, the Irish Exiles League of Great Britain in attracting support. In December 1922 the Republicans had 26 affiliated clubs, there were 30 the following month and by May the total had risen to 34.[4] By contrast the Free State body does not seem to have expanded beyond the Airdrie and Coatbridge areas.[5] Cumann Poblacht na hÉireann faded from view and was replaced once more by Sinn Féin in 1924.

Countess Markievicz in the uniform of the Irish Citizen Army.

A major function of Cumann Poblacht na hÉireann was to disseminate the Republican viewpoint. This task was fulfilled not only by sponsoring prominent Republicans to give lecture tours, but also by the publication of newspapers. The first of these was *Poblacht na hÉireann* (Scottish edition) which was later superseded by *Éire*. The columns of the former publication gave details of club activities and public meetings, carried many appeals for donations, outlined the success and difficulties encountered by Republicans when attempting to further the cause amongst the Irish community and printed many articles about alleged Free State atrocities. The newspaper was successful and had a large readership amongst the London Irish and subscribers from as far away as Barcelona. [6]

Of those who were high-ranking pre-Treaty Sinn Féin and IRA officials in Scotland who remained active, the majority backed the anti-Treaty cause.

For the IRA the main task was to acquire as much weaponry as possible and smuggle it to the anti-Treaty forces in Ireland. The sources of supply were the same as those used during the War of Independence. Continental Europe was scoured for arms and a link was established with sympathisers in Hamburg.[7] In Scotland colliery armouries and rifle ranges were raided by anti-Treaty forces. As before the Treaty the majority of arms acquired in Scotland were smuggled to Ireland via Liverpool though on one occasion, a steamer travelling to Sligo from Glasgow was discovered to be carrying arms destined for the Republican forces.[8] A lot of arms and ammunition ended up in the Rosses district of Donegal where family links with the Irish in the west of Scotland were strong.

∴ **Óglaigh na hÉireann** ∴

DEPT.........................

REF. No...................

HEADQUARTERS,
1st SCOTTISH BRIGADE,
GLASGOW.

Scottish Brigade IRA letter heading.

There is evidence that the IRA in Scotland sent members over to Ireland to fight against the Free State forces. In a notice printed in *Poblacht na hÉireann* (Scottish edition) it was announced that a

Comforts Fund Committee was formed with the intention of aiding the Glasgow IRA Expeditionary Force in Ireland.[9]

A young Scottish Gael who took the Republican side in the Civil War was Ian MacKenzie Kennedy ("Scottie") from Inverness-shire. In 1916 he went to Ireland in a quest for the Irish language and later joined the West Cork Brigade of the IRA. He was killed by Free State forces near Passage West in August 1922 whilst defending the Republic.[10]

Earlier in one of the most famous episodes of the War of Independence, the Crossbarry ambush in 19 March 1921, another Scottish born volunteer in the West Cork Brigade known as 'Peter Monahan', was shot and killed.[11] Three Scots named William Williamson, Donald McInnes and John Lynn who joined the Free State Army were killed by the IRA in the Civil War.

143

Some members of the Free State Army, anxious to sever the Scottish connection as a source of aid to its enemies, worked as intelligence agents in Scotland, monitoring the activities of their Republican counterparts. Consequently the British intelligence services and the police had a much clearer picture of who was involved in the Republican Movement by the time of the Civil War.

Shortly before the close of the Civil War in March 1923, the British authorities arrested 110 Republican activists in Scotland and England in an effort to shut down their activities. Of the 38 arrested in Scotland, 28 were from Glasgow, 6 from Lanarkshire, 1 from Dunbartonshire, 2 from West Lothian and 1 was from Dundee. They were illegally deported to Ireland on the destroyer 'Wolfhound' and handed over to Free State soldiers who interned them in Mountjoy Jail in Dublin. Four of them were women who were members of the Anne Devlin Branch of Cumann na mBan in Glasgow. There was a wave of protests from Independent Labour Party branches (copies of their letters being found in the file on 'Irish disturbances' in the National Archives of Scotland) and questions were asked in parliament by ILP MP James Maxton, the Communist Indian MP Shapurji Saklatvala and others. It was stressed that many of those deported to Ireland were in fact of English and Scottish birth with a few having no Irish ancestry at all. In October 1923 a total of £17,000 was awarded to the Scottish deportees but they never collected it.

After the Civil War, the Republican Movement's activity in Scotland went into decline as the spectacle of Irishman killing Irishman weakened Irish political and cultural movements. There was none of the life or the adventure in Sinn Féin that was evident in the preceding years. Many of the volunteers returned to Ireland and joined their local Companies. Some stayed in Scotland for good, especially those who were born and raised there, and did their best to maintain an Irish identity through membership of the Republican Movement or by going into the Gaelic League or the Gaelic Athletic Association. Others were so disappointed with the split that they simply left the Republican Movement altogether and some went on to join the labour movement and the Scottish nationalists.

Frank Carty

Within days of his attempted rescue Frank Carty was brought in charge of an imposing RIC escort to Dublin and lodged in C3 Mountjoy Jail. He was later court-martialled in Kilmainham Jail on charges of having escaped from Sligo Prison, from Derry Prison and having an RIC revolver and 5 rounds of ammunition in his possession when captured at Moylough in County Sligo. He was sentenced to ten years penal servitude but was released during the Truce in August 1921.

His homecoming to his native Sligo was a memorable event. When the train conveying him came to a halt at Carrowmore station, he was greeted by a salute from over three hundred Volunteers and by the cheers of his many supporters and admirers who had travelled from far and wide to greet him.

On the outbreak of the Civil War, Frank Carty threw himself wholeheartedly on the Anti-Treaty side. His speech at a Tubbercurry anti-Treaty meeting at the end of February 1922 dealt with both the Republic and the oath. He mentioned what he regarded as the 'real issue', "When we were elected...we were elected as Republicans and not as Free Staters or Home Rulers". Mentioning the oath of allegiance to the Republic he said, "The oath I regard as sacred and binding and I will not swear another oath pledging fealty to the British king...The spirit of the Republic is unconquerable". He concluded by asserting that the people of Tubbercurry would stand by "the Republic proclaimed by the men of Easter Week, sanctified by their blood and ratified and legalised by two general elections". What the Treaty granted was less than a Republic and would result in less freedom for Ireland, he said, claiming the "so-called Treaty would give Ireland merely a mutilated dominion status and make the Irish subjects of the British crown". For Carty, acceptance of the Treaty meant becoming "West Britons" and "crawling slaves in the British Empire". *The Connachtman* claimed that the Free State was, "simply the British Government masquerading in a new disguise". [12]

The three successful anti-Treaty candidates at the June 1922 election, Seamus Devins (left), Dr Francis Ferran (second from right) and Frank Carty (right). Michael Nevin, Mayor of Sligo, is second from the left.

Frank Carty was to become the most prominent Republican leader in County Sligo and was the Officer in Command of the South Sligo Brigade. In this role he was to lead numerous military engagements with former comrades in the Free State Army.

Seán Adair

A sensational sequel to the prison van episode was to be enacted on 13th July 1922 in County Sligo. Seán Adair, who had joined the Free State Army, was on his way to Athlone to visit his mother, who he had not seen for a considerable time. He was one of the 13 men arrested in the church hall in Tollcross. En route, he joined a party of Free State troops that had a post in Markree Castle. Escorted by the *Ballinalee* armoured car, Free State troops left the new post at 6am, bound for Sligo. Captain Michael Robinson travelled in charge of the armoured car, whilst his commanding officer, Commandant Paddy Callaghan, was with the majority of the men in the lorry. As they approached Dooney Rock, they were stopped by a roadblock, when immediately the ambushers opened fire. The first volley killed

Callaghan and a young volunteer from Longford, Sergeant John Farrell. Captain Robinson got out of the armoured car and the ambushers captured it. With its Vickers gun it was a formidable weapon in the hands of the Republicans.

Seán Adair

The *Ballinalee* was not surrendered without a hard fight in which Quartermaster Seán Adair was killed and another volunteer, Sweeney, fatally wounded.[13] The irony of the circumstances of Adair's death was that the men who killed him were under the command of Brigadier Frank Carty whom Adair had attempted to rescue in the attack on the prison van.[14]

The political career of Frank Carty was no less distinguished than his military record. He was first elected to the Second Dáil for East Mayo and South Sligo whilst in Mountjoy Jail in 1921 at the age of twenty-five and was known as the 'Babe' of the House. At the General Election of 1923 he was elected for the Sligo-Leitrim constituency. In common with other TDs opposed to the Anglo-Irish Treaty, he upheld the abstentionist policy and did not take his seat until August 1927, when he followed de Valera into Leinster House as a founder member of Fianna Fáil. He was returned with an increased majority in each of the subsequent general elections until 1938.

Frank Carty also played an active role in local politics. Elected a member of the first Republican County Council during his imprisonment in 1920, he was chairman of that body from 1928-1934.

Carty was virtually self-educated, and, in addition to his farming interests, he studied law and was called to the Bar at King's Inn's in 1936. He was described as a forceful and eloquent speaker and possessed of a keen intellect, qualities he used to the best advantage in the law courts, Leinster House and the local councils. He died in September 1942 at the age of forty-five. [15]

A fine Celtic cross over his final resting place in Anchory cemetery bears the following inscription:

To the memory of
Frank Carty,
Barrister-at-Law, T.D.
3rd Western Division, I.R.A.,
who died September 10th, 1942,
aged 45.
Ard Dheis De go raibh a anam

Éamonn Mooney

Éamonn Mooney as we have seen was arrested while "on the run" with his brother Seaghan in Edinburgh, when arrangements were being made by the IRB to get them both to Germany prior to their intended departure to the United States. They were later released as part of a general amnesty for Republican prisoners after the Treaty was signed and went on active service in Ireland and were later captured. According to the British authorities, Mooney was "very active and dangerous" and was wanted by the Free State authorities for escaping from Dundalk Barracks after the 4th Northern Division of the IRA recaptured it on 14th August 1922, in what was one of the Republican coups of the war. He spent some time in South Africa promoting the Republican position and returned to Scotland while "on the run" and helped R Scott Hayward alias George Humphries produce the *Irish Nation* and *Éire*. These newspapers helped to keep alive the national spirit and were sold in various Irish outlets including shops belonging to Miss Kearney and Liam Gribben (fought in the 1916 Rising as a member of the Scottish Division) on High Street. Mooney was arrested with other prominent Republicans in

Commandant Éamonn Mooney

March 1923, deported to Dublin and incarcerated in Mountjoy Jail. He later went to Manchester where he was attached to the Department of Publicity under P. J. Little who was to become Minister of Posts and Telegraphs in de Valera's 1939 government.

When Fianna Fáil came into power in 1932 Éamonn was given a public works job. He married and had a family and worked for the Scottish veterans of the IRA on the Military Service Pensions Board. He died on 18th June 1965 having been prominently associated with the National Movement in Ireland, England, Scotland and the United States for over 50 years.

Seaghan Mooney

Seaghan took an active part in the Irish Civil War on the Republican side. He was an assistant to Oscar Traynor, the Commandant of the IRA in Dublin City where about three-quarters of the Brigade staff defended the Republic. His subsequent arrest and detention by the Free State forces was reported in an article that appeared in the 14th October 1922 edition of *Poblacht na hÉireann* (Scottish edition) under the heading 'Young Man's Trying Ordeal'. It reads as follows:

> "A young Volunteer (Seaghan Mooney), well known in Irish circles in Glasgow, was arrested about the latter end of September by the C.I.D. in the South Dublin area and taken to the Naval Base, Dun Laoghaire where he had to undergo a most agonising and brutal ordeal at the hands of Churchill's 'Green and Tans.'[16] First they questioned him with regard to a bomb that had been thrown into a house occupied by some C.I.D. men which they blamed him for throwing. He told them he didn't throw it. They then asked him about the officers, ammunition dumps, etc. but he would give no information. At midnight they took him out and questioned him again. They told him he was a 'looked for man', and that he was going to be shot, put him against a low wall, and told him to say his prayers. He did so. Then they fired 4 or 5 shots around him. One bullet passed over his head, but he never winced. All he said was 'Damned bad shot.' They could not help but admire his coolness. One Free State Officer then asked him his record in the past. He told them he had been in prison in connection with the attack on the Glasgow prison van, on hearing which the officer began to cry over him (drink of course), and said, I'll throw off my coat.' The prisoner was then moved to Wellington Barracks, 'another well known torture chamber,' where he is at present incarcerated. It may be mentioned he also had the honour of

150

being in action in company with the noble hero, the late Cathal Brugha R.I.P."

He later spent a number of years working in America. Mooney was later incarcerated in the Curragh Internment Camp in County Kildare for his Republican activities. He later undertook printing work for Emanuel Shinwell one of the 'Red Clydeside' MPs. He subsequently got married, had a family and secured a job with the civil service in Dublin. He ended his days working as a harbour constable in Dun Laoghaire and died of a heart attack on 26 July 1970 aged 67. He is buried with his wife in Deansgrange Cemetery. A modest man, Seaghan rarely spoke about his involvement in the IRA except in the company of old comrades.

Michael O'Carroll

This section is based on interviews that journalist John Cooney conducted with Michael O'Carroll in various locations following their chance meeting in the County Sligo village of Easkey in August 1985.[17] O'Carroll was born in Dublin in 1901. His father, a carpenter, was from Inniskeen, County Monaghan. His mother, Margaret Healy, from County Meath, was a cousin of Joe Brady, a member of the secret society, the Invincibles, who was hung for the killings in Dublin's Phoenix Park in 1882 of the Chief Secretary to Ireland, Lord Frederick Cavendish, and the Permanent Secretary, Thomas Henry Burke. One of four boys and three sisters, Mick grew up in a strong Republican household. The first photograph was taken of him in 1906 wearing a sailor-like hat with the words *Sinn Féin* embroidered on its rim.

In 1912 O'Carroll joined the Willie Nelson Slua of Na Fianna Éireann in Glasgow where he met other like-minded young lads including Éamonn and Seaghan Mooney. He also attended Fianna meetings in Dublin's Hardwicke Street under the captaincy of Seán Heuston. There he met Willie Pearse and Con Colbert both to be executed at Kilmainham in May 1916. He witnessed the 1913 Dublin Lock-out.

'I saw the baton charges in O'Connell Street. I can remember quite vividly Jim Larkin and all the members of the Citizen's Army, the lockout and the Labour agitation. I remember Madame Maud Gonne MacBride and the women along the

151

Liffey quay handing out parcels of food which came from the trade union workers' organisations in England. It was in this spirit and atmosphere that I grew up as a kid. The Dublin Metropolitan Police held sway. The workers were batoned off the streets. So were their wives and children. Prams were upset. It was a rough time. History records that in 1913 Dublin was the most underfed city in Europe.'

O'Carroll immigrated to Glasgow in 1917, took up digs in Bridgeton and secured a job in the Trongate. Every Saturday he attended Irish dances at the Old Hibernian in London Bridge Road where he met Joseph Robinson who swore him into the IRB as its youngest member.

'I was assigned to move out to different places particularly at the weekend in the mining districts. Joe Robinson accompanied me and introduced me. Each week I would return to Glasgow with a package weighing up to seven or ten pounds in gelignite. This was stored in a little place in the Saltmarket. You would be amazed at the amount of stuff. I made frequent trips to Dublin bringing parcels and containers with me. There was always a consignment for the Citizen Army always one for the Volunteers.'

'Things were beginning to shape up. The Volunteers were forming companies all over Glasgow and the West of Scotland. Sinn Féin was taking on great proportions. I was now working in the Trongate in a brush shop. Barney McCabe, a businessman (fought with the Scottish Division in the 1916 Rising) accommodated us in every way. The arms began to flow in and we established dumps where these arms could be safely secured. We got cooperation from people who were not connected with the movement but who were militant ILP. At that time they were gathering arms too and we bought arms from them. They did have an idea of a physical movement in Scotland to bring about social revolution.[18] Dumps were fairly well established throughout Glasgow, in Dumbarton, Wishaw and Uddingston, and other places. Places which recall to mind, where I gathered a lot of stuff and there were a lot of company volunteers, were Leith, Stirling, Dumfries, Hamilton, Blantyre, Bothwell, Carfin and Dundee. O'Carroll spoke highly of Henry Coyle and Joe Vize.'

152

'As the arms came in we shipped them in a commercial way to Dublin. Those arms usually went to Liverpool. They were reassigned from Liverpool to Dublin. We were working in conjunction with London and Liverpool. Neill Kerr who was an important figure in customs and excise, fairly organised things.'

The supply of arms became more prolific after the Armistice in the Great War in November 1918.

'There was a lot of stuff knocking about – rifles Webleys; lads home on leave. The money was pouring in and we had the money to buy stuff. We were now sending the stuff across with passengers in diverse ways – on cattle boats and other ships. We found out at different ceili from different girls where they were working. If they were in offices shipping material to Ireland especially to Dublin we were able to get samples of their invoices and billheads. We started shipping stuff to Dublin from Glasgow. The main artery was Tommy Tracey an undertaker. Tommy had a branch in Parkhead where we packed the stuff. That place was never tapped'.

Tracey and his wife Mary were arrested for alleged involvement in the attempt to rescue Frank Carty and were acquitted at the trial.

O'Carroll maintained his allegiance to the Republic and along with other comrades in Scotland was deported to Dublin in March 1923 and held in Mountjoy Jail. In 1949 O'Carroll is recorded as having delivered a paper to the Old IRA Literary and Debating Society on the theme of the Scottish Brigade of the IRA. According to the *Dublin Evening Mail (28/11/1949)* 'Not only was it full of information but it was an almost complete refutation of a book on the Irish in Scotland which has been subsidised by the National University of Ireland.' The article went on to state 'but then Mr O'Carroll knew his facts and did not rely on the accounts in the "enemy" press'.[19] Several decades later O'Carroll returned to Glasgow on a visit and went to the site of the ambush where he had his photograph taken standing beside the bullet holes in the remains of the prison wall. He ended his days in Lurganboy in County Leitrim and died in the late 1980s.

Seán Flood

Seán Flood was involved in the attempt to spring Frank Carty from the prison van. He left Dublin in 1919 for Glasgow where he was appointed Quartermaster of the 1st Battalion of the Scottish Brigade raiding for arms and fundraising for same, delivering the proceeds to Michael Collins. He subsequently helped to found the Scottish Brigade Old IRA Association and held the office of Financial Secretary for 25 years. He lived in Dalkey in County Dublin and died on 8 November 1960 aged 65.

Andrew Fagan

Andrew Fagan who participated in the attempted rescue was one of the 18 people released in July 1921 for lack of evidence to convict him. Born in County Meath Andy Fagan was the eldest of sixteen children of the marriage of Matthew Fagan and Bridget Hoey. After eviction from their small farm at Kingscourt, the Fagans moved to the United States, but stayed only for a year before returning to Meath. Unsettled, especially after the death of his first wife, Andy moved to Scotland, where his first job was in Ardeer with I.C.I where he was tutored in the use of explosives. He moved to Blantyre to work in the pits but, finding it increasingly difficult to obtain work, he became involved in politics and union work. Fagan fought injustice wherever he saw it, filling in forms, advising people of their rights, going to rent tribunals with them. He was an activist who incurred the anger and ill will of the bosses.

In 1919, at the Gaelic Hall in Blantyre, Fagan was host to Countess Markievicz. Clandestine overnight visitors in his home in John Street included Liam Mellows and Dan Breen.

Andrew Fagan became Quartermaster of the Scottish Brigade of the IRA and in 1920 or 1921 travelled to Ireland to interview Michael Collins at a time when it is claimed there was a reward of £20,000 for the capture of Collins. Fagan was believed to have set up an almost fail-proof system for getting arms and ensuring they were safely transported to Ireland. He had numerous contacts in Irish clubs, business circles, dock areas, sailors, workers' and even within the military establishment where some were privately sympathetic to the Irish cause. He never used the same contacts regularly but instead used a rota to fool the police. He was very cautious, very careful. Brigade Quartermaster Andrew Fagan along with Brigade Transport Officer Henry Coyle and Commandant Joseph Vize were responsible for the successful raid on the 6th Scottish Rifles Military Barracks at Hamilton in 1919.[20]

Andrew Fagan is second on the left in the middle row and John MacLean is in the middle of the front row of this photograph of students of the Scottish Labour College in 1920-21.

In 1920 Fagan was awarded a scholarship by the Lanarkshire Miners Union to enable promising members to avail themselves of a course of study at the Scottish Labour College run by John MacLean. Fagan had little or no schooling and arithmetic and algebra were foreign to him when he came to Scotland aged 17. But in the most difficult subjects such as trying to get an understanding of Dietzgen's *Science of Understanding* and *Philosophy*, on which John MacLean lectured and which were required reading, Fagan was the outstanding pupil of the college.[21] Shortly before he died in 1975, the firm for which he worked for fifty years recommended him for a British Empire Medal from the Queen as the oldest working man in Scotland. Although then 89, Fagan was still doing manual work for five days a week for Murdoch Mackenzie Ltd, a civil engineering and construction firm based in Motherwell. His award attracted extensive media coverage as he obligingly celebrated with a quick flip on his motor scooter – with a glass of whisky in hand. But as Fagan posed for photos for the press, the story that was missed was that this particular recipient of the Queen's Award was the proud holder of a Service Medal for his IRA activities in Scotland.[22]

Seámus Fullerton

Seámus Fullerton stayed in Turner Street in the Garngad district of Glasgow where many Irish people lived. He married Mary Simpson and had five of a family. James held the rank of First Lieutenant of B Company of the 1st Battalion of the Irish Volunteers at the time of the 1916 Rising. He later became Commandant of the 1st Battalion and took an active part in the attempt to free Frank Carty. Fullerton later heeded an order by Michael Collins instructing members of the Scottish Brigade to support the newly formed Free State and join the Irish National Army. He was in fact its most senior officer in Scotland. When the Civil War was over James went to Staten Island in New York intending that his wife and family should join him. However he did not settle in America and went to Ireland instead.

He was appointed general manager of a boot factory in Emyvale in County Monaghan. The factory was to close and Seámus and his family moved to County Waterford where he worked as a factory manager for several years. Around 1953 the family moved to Dublin where he found employment in Castleknock College as a bursar after his official retirement. Around this time he was Chairman of the Scottish Brigade Old IRA Association although had to temporarily stand down due to business commitments. Seámus died in Dublin in 1987 aged 88 and is buried in Balgriffin Cemetery.

Liam Fullerton

Liam Fullerton married Chrissie Little and they had eight of a family and lived in the Balornock area of Glasgow. Liam served with his brother Seámus in B Company of the First Battalion of the IRA. With his brother, sister Susan and his mother Susan (nee Hegarty), they joined an estimated half million people who turned out for the funeral of Michael Collins in Dublin. In the 1920s Liam worked as a travelling salesman for the Singer sewing machine company. In later years he worked at the Caledonia Railway Works in Springburn. He died in 1981 and is buried in St. Kentigern's Cemetery in Lambhill, Glasgow.[23]

Father MacRory

Father Patrick MacRory.

As we have seen, Father MacRory received a hero's welcome after his release from Duke Street Prison in July 1921. A committee was soon set up and a presentation organised in his honour. Contributions flowed in from the parish of St Mary's, and indeed from all over Glasgow and the rest of Scotland. Fr Pat's mother and sister were guests of honour at the presentation in St Mary's Hall, which was thronged by the Irish Catholics of Glasgow, who wished to pay tribute to their young curate, whom they felt had been so cruelly treated. A costly chalice and a substantial cheque were presented to "Glasgow's most popular citizen." The chalice, made of silver and dipped in gold, had P.S. MacRory engraved on it.

Father Pat, acknowledging the presentation, said, "Politically, as a Sinn Feiner, I have nothing to complain of, I got just what was expected from British police and I can mention the names of other priests - Canon Magner, Father Griffin and others - who received harsher treatment. [24] As a priest I have to complain of the sacrilege. The authorities of Glasgow did not know what they were doing when they arrested me before 12 o'clock that night they knew it...I will never forget the kindness of the priests and people of Glasgow".

But despite the joy that followed Father MacRory's release from prison, his story was not to have a happy ending.

He died less than three years later after surgery for appendicitis on April 11th 1924.

The *Glasgow Observer* reported:

> "News of Father MacRory's demise swept through the city and many Irish hearts mourned. His sensational arrest on May 4 1921 was recalled and his unjustifiable incarceration for eleven weeks without trial.
>
> He was the type of priest who hid under a cheerful mask, a shy and retiring nature. His only loves were God and his people while he confessed an enthusiasm for sport. All during the three nights preceding his demise his faithful people besieged heaven with prayers for his recovery. All night vigils in the church were observed by thousands of St Mary's parishioners. But in vain Sogarth Aroon had to go to his God."

158

The Ulster Herald added:

"It can be truly said that no priest in the Archdiocese of Glasgow was more fondly esteemed and it is equally true that the sorrow occasioned by his early demise is nowhere, outside the members of his own family, more intense than amongst those for whom he worked unselfishly in the city by the Clyde."

On the morning of April 12th, the remains were removed from St Vincent's Nursing Home to St Mary's where Requiem Mass was celebrated. Afterwards the coffin, in the presence of a huge cortege, was brought to the quays for the last journey back to Ireland. At Derry a large crowd from Omagh district met the remains for the sad journey back to Tyrone. Along the route people gathered to pay their final respects. Near Omagh a huge crowd had gathered on the Derry Road and walked in procession to the Sacred Heart Church, where the remains were placed on a catafalque. During the afternoon there was a constant stream on sympathisers offering their prayers for the repose of his soul.

On 14th May, Very Rev. Philip O'Doherty, P.P.,V.F., presided at Solemn Office and Requiem High Mass. Appropriately the celebrant was Fr. E Fitzgerald, rector of St Mary's parish, Glasgow and who had been Fr. Pat's sincere friend, especially during the period of his arrest and incarceration.

Very Rev. Philip O'Doherty.

159

After Mass a touching oration was preached by Very Rev. Philip O'Doherty, after which the funeral took place at St Mary's, Killyclogher.

Father MacRory's grave in St Mary's Churchyard, Killyclogher.

From the *Glasgow Observer*, April 19th, 1924:

TO THE MEMORY OF FATHER MACRORY

In the springtime of life as I knew you
The future seemed lovely and fair
In the heart of this city of sorrow and strife
The fruits of your labours were there.

Bereft of your guidance and counsel
Our sorrow is hard to restrain,
And our hearts seek to reach you, dear Soggarth Aroon
In the peace of your happy domain.   – J.P.R. (Mile End)

The memory of Father Pat is still cherished amongst the Glasgow Irish, especially in the parish he loved. On the 70th anniversary of his death in December 1994 the Glasgow Irish community placed memorial notices in local newspapers. The journalist Frank Dolan retold the story of how Fr. MacRory rose to prominence in an *Irish Post* column titled 'When Glasgow Re-enacted the Manchester Martyrs Story'. Fittingly, a Mass, parts of which were said in Gaelic, was held in St Mary's Church in Abercromby Street on 12th December. Representatives of various Irish bodies were present and a choir from the Gaelic League sang several hymns in Irish.

St Mary's Church, Abercromby Street, Calton.

Canon Bernard J Canning gave the homily on the theme of immigration. He traced the 150th year of the Great Hunger being observed in 1995, the development of the Irish emigrants and Irish-born secular priests in Scotland in the 150 years after Catholic Emancipation in 1829 and how every diocese in Ireland gave priests on loan to Scotland. He spoke of Fr. MacRory's four short years at St Mary's, Calton, the cradle of Catholicism in Glasgow, then a busy parish served by six priests; his imprisonment for close on twelve weeks; all night vigils by the people at St Mary's, their joy at his release; and the sorrow at his death three years later of appendicitis. [25]

The author had an appeal for information about Father MacRory published in Glasgow newspapers in 1993 and received several replies from former parishioners, who despite having been very young, were able to remember him and wrote fondly about their young curate. Several mentioned that Father Pat's photograph hung on the wall of many Irish families' homes in the east end of the city.

Detective Sergeant George Stirton

DS Stirton lived with his wife in Springburn until his retirement from the force in 1936. He later moved to Ayr where he died in 1957. Due to the politics of the time, neither DS Stirton nor Detective Constable Macdonald was decorated for their bravery during the attack on the prison van. DC Macdonald was later promoted to the post of Chief Constable of the Lanarkshire Constabulary.[26]

Reunion of Survivors of the Glasgow Smashing of the Van

The Dublin based *Sunday Press* newspaper carried an interesting item in its edition dated 27 February 1955. It announced that the 'Prison van raid will be recalled' and stated that only 12 remaining participants were still alive and that one of the prominent officers involved in the rescue attempt, 56 year old Dublin businessman, Seámus Fullerton would attend. The talk was organised by the veterans of Seán Óglaigh na h-Éireann Briogáid na h-Albáin (Scottish Brigade Old IRA Association) and was delivered by Éamonn De Barra to a packed audience at 196 Pearse Street in Dublin. [27] Unfortunately the author was unable to locate a report of the talk.[28]

Celtic Cross Erected In Memory of the Overseas Units of the IRA

Following a meeting of surviving members of the overseas units of the Irish Republican Army including members of the Scottish Brigade from the Tan War period, a granite headstone in the shape of a Celtic cross was erected over two plots in St Fintan's Cemetery in

Sutton, County Dublin in the early 1960s. Buried there, are Éamonn Mooney and Seán Flood who both took part in the rescue attempt, and Patrick Ryan of the Liverpool IRA. The inscription reads:

The Overseas Units of the
Irish Republican Army
In memory of their comrades
Who served in the
Fight for Freedom
R.I.P.

Overseas Units of the IRA Plot, St Fintan's Cemetery, Sutton, County Dublin.

The Van

"I Discover a 'Ghost' in East Kilbride" was the heading of a remarkable story that was published in the 31st March 1961 edition of the Glasgow *Evening Citizen*. The story's author, Neil Stuart, commented, "I've been out to East Kilbride to see a ghost - the faded, scarred remains of a Black Maria that was in the headlines 40 years ago when Sinn Fein bullets ripped into it in Glasgow's High Street."

Mr James Stewart beside the door of the Black Maria at Craigmill near East Kilbride in 1961.

He continues, "Grey Duke Street prison was the backcloth then. Today the setting is richer and greener, for the Black Maria, built into a weekend hut, stands in a field close to hencoops beside ancient Craigmill water mill. Mr James Stewart, the present miller, who showed the bullet scars in the door, does not know how the van with the turbulent history got to East Kilbride or when it arrived. But it has been used by a succession of families who have enjoyed weekends, possibly unaware that their shelter was once a target for vicious gunmen and that a policeman had been shot." He then went on to summarise the ambush story.

The author followed up the story in a telephone call to the widow of Mr Stewart in December 1993. She remembered the newspaper story and was aware of the significance of the prison van, which was one of four Thorneycroft models acquired by the Glasgow police force. She recalled that the van was sold at auction and was purchased by a Mr James Tenant who had lived in Carntyne. She believed the van was brought to Craigmill sometime between 1928 and the early 1930s.

Mrs E Stewart actually slept in the van and found it comfortable. She remembered the iron bars still being on the windows. The huts were popular and were mainly used at New Year. It was customary for men to sleep in tents and for the women to occupy the huts. Mrs Stewart stated that a woman called Betty Tenant was the last person to use it.

As a result of the newspaper story, souvenir hunters would show up and remove splinters of wood from the van. The holiday huts went out of fashion and the hut fell into ruin and was vandalised. The huts closed around 1974 or 1975 and the van would have been disposed of. [29]

The Ballad

The 'Smashing of the Van' (*Appendix 2*) is immortalised in a street ballad of the Glasgow Irish. The late Mick McLaughlan, a native of the Garngad district of the city, wrote the song. He was a well-known raconteur, poet, songwriter, practical joker and a popular figure at wakes. Mick Garngad, as he was affectionately known, was also the author of the famous 'Ballad of James Connolly' as well as a string of Glasgow Celtic songs including 'The Celtic Song', 'The Johnny Thompson Song' and the 'Coronation Cup Song'. [30]

The Smashing of the Van was published in the 1967 edition of the Rebel Ceilidh Song Book. This is a collector's item and contains a foreword by Hugh MacDiarmid the acclaimed Scottish poet. The ballad was also published in 'The Songs of Past and People 11' by

Dreoilin Community Arts in association with Mid-West Radio and Knock Folk Museum in County Mayo.[31] In January 1981 the ballad was broadcast on Radio Éireann from Wexford. The Irish Brigade who recorded the Smashing of the Van mistakenly give the date of the ambush as the 12th of May and miss out the third verse of the song.

The forbidding building that was Duke Street Prison was demolished to make way for the Ladywell flats in the 1950s. The cut-down remains of the boundary wall survived the bulldozers but the reduction removed the stones in which bullets were visibly lodged. Bullet holes can still be seen in the lower section of the wall where the ambush occurred. The late Glasgow historian, Jack House, liked to make a point of taking visitors up the High Street and of telling them his version of the rescue bid. He would then invite them to put a finger in an IRA bullet hole. He states that, "At the end of the day, when I had shown them the wonders of this wonderful city, I would ask them what impressed them most. Almost invariably each would reply, 'Putting a finger into a bullet hole in the wall of Duke Street Prison' ".[32]

Remains of the old prison wall at corner of High Street and Burrell's Lane where the bullet holes are still visible. Immediately behind the wall is the site of the gallows.

The ambush site as it looks today. The remains of the prison wall can be seen on the left of the photograph and on the opposite side of the road only a remnant of the Hydraulic Water Pumping Station building is left standing.

Notes

1. Quoted in *Sinn Féin 100 years of Revolution 1905-2005*, Des Dalton, Irish Freedom Press, Dublin, 2005, p.18.
2. A series of articles looking at the role of McPeak in the death of Collins were published in the 12, 13 and 14 September 1996 editions of the (Glasgow) *Herald*.
3. Several Republicans with Scottish addresses were arrested following the seizure of the Four Courts.
4. Ian D Patterson, *The Impact of the Irish Revolution in the Irish Community in Scotland, 1916-23'*, M.Phil, thesis, University of Strathclyde, 1993, p.222.
5. *Glasgow Observer*, 23 December 1922.
6. Patterson, op cit, p.229.
7. Patterson, op cit, p.230.
8. Patterson, op cit, p.230.
9. Patterson, op cit, p.230.
10. For more information on Ian MacKenzie Kennedy see 'A Scottish Gael Who Died for the Irish Republic' by Stephen Coyle, *Ballingeary Historical Society Journal*, 2006, pp.4-6.

11. 'Peter Monahan' who was a mining engineer, deserted from the Cameron Highlanders with another soldier from their base in Cobh. He became a trusted and valued member of the IRA. His real identity remains unknown and he was referred to as "the unknown soldier". He is buried in the cemetery above Bandon under his assumed name.

12. Quoted in Farry, Michael, *The Aftermath of Revolution: Sligo 1921-23*, University College of Dublin Press, 2000, p.45.

13. Report of ambush in *Ireland's Civil War*, by Calton Younger, Glasgow 1982, pp.362-363.

14. Reports of the killing of Seán Adair appeared in the *Glasgow Herald*, ' Sean O'Dair, A Dramatic End, Glasgow Outrage Recalled', 22 July 1921; *Glasgow Observer*, 'Glasgow IRA Man Killed, Sean Adair Falls in Sligo Ambush', 29 July 1922.

15. See the *The Roscommon Herald* dated 29 August 1942, for biographical details of Frank Carty. See Farry for details of his Civil War activities.

16. This was a derisory term used by Republicans to describe the Free State army.

17. John Cooney, 'The Irish Republican Brotherhood in Scotland: The Untold Stories of Andrew Fagan and Michael O'Carroll', *Celebrating Columba: Irish Scottish Connections 597-1997*, TM Devine and JF McMillan (eds.), John Donald, Edinburgh, 1999, pp.138-154.

18. In response to John MacLean's call to stop the deployment of Scottish troops against their fellow Gaels in Ireland, a Scottish nationalist military body was formed called Fianna na h-Alba. It contemplated military action for the liberation of Scotland. Whilst little is known about this episode, correspondence between Michael Collins and Art O'Brien, the leader of the Irish Self Determination League in England, would indicate that Ruaridh Erskine of Mar and William Gillies were involved. Collins was sceptical about their prospects and in a letter dated 21 March 1921 comments, "they do not appreciate the particular difficulties they are up against." He observed that the Irish were stronger even during their weakest period (1904 to 1908) than they (Scottish nationalists) seem to be at present; regarded the issuing of a proclamation premature and felt it better to work away as a handful than generate false hopes. "Failure in this manner would mean much more to the small groups than years of tireless labour and non-recognition". In any event possibly due to advice from the Irish, Fianna na h-Alba abandoned its plans.

19. Presumably this is a reference to *The Irish in Modern Scotland* by James E. Handley which was published in Cork in1947.

168

Handley wrongly gives the year of the Glasgow ambush in his book as 1920 instead of 1921.

20. For the Hamilton raid six men were selected from the Lanarkshire companies. One of the IRA's main contact men within the barracks was a shoemaker who repaired boots and saddlery for the military. He supplied full particulars of where the rifles were stored and succeeded in procuring a key that would give the raiding party access to the stores concerned. On the night of the raid six Volunteers succeeded in getting over the wall of the military barracks and entered the stores, with the key in their possession. This was an easy matter and in about twenty minutes about 75 Lee Enfield rifles and bayonets were handed out over the wall to the remainder of the raiding party who were ready to take the rifles away. A lorry was standing by and the rifles were loaded onto it. The lorry travelled to Liverpool and it was actually back in Hamilton before the military authorities discovered their loss. (This account is contained in a statement by James Byrne, NAI, BMH papers, WS 828, pp.4-5).

21. Iain McDougall (editor), *Militant Miners*, Edinburgh, 1981, p.35.

22. John Cooney, 'The Irish Republican Brotherhood in Scotland: The Untold Stories of Andrew Fagan and Michael O'Carroll', *Celebrating Columba: Irish Scottish Connections 597-1997*, TM Devine and JF McMillan (eds.), John Donald, Edinburgh, 1999, p.144; John Cooney, 'IRA Man Andy, a royal medal and the road to an era of peace', Irish Press, 29 April 1989.

23. I am grateful to Jim Friel for supplying me with this information about Seámus and Liam Fullerton. Susan Hegarty claimed to be a descendant of Michael Larkin who as one of the Manchester Martyrs was allegedly involved in the original 'smashing of the van'.

24. Canon Magner was killed by the Black and Tans on 15 December 1920, for refusing to toll the bell of his chapel in Dunmanway in County Cork, on Armistice Day. Father Griffin was found in a bog with a bullet wound to his head, in Bearna, County Galway in November 1920. It was done to silence him as he was due to go to America to give evidence to a commission of inquiry that was set up to investigate conditions in Ireland. See *The Irish Republic* by Dorothy Macardle, Victor Gollancz, London, 1968, p.32, pp.383-384.

25. See report of Mass titled 'Father Pat Remembered', in *Scottish Catholic Observer*, 23 December 1994.

26. Information supplied by the Glasgow Police Museum which is located in the former Central Police Court in Turnbull Street.

27. The Scottish Brigade Old IRA Association was formed as a result of the Military Service Act of 1934 and continued until the

169

mid 1960s. Serving officers from the period 1916-23 overcame the divisions of the Civil War and met primarily to deal with applications from former comrades for pensions and service medals to which they were entitled. Most of the membership was based in Dublin city and county although they extended throughout the Irish Diaspora, especially Scotland. The Association gathered for an annual reunion dinner and Mass and helped its members to live their lives in the State they helped to establish. Among its more notable activities was the commissioning of a portrait painting of Commandant General Joseph Robinson of the Scottish Brigade which was accepted by Dr. Hayes-McCoy of the National Museum on behalf of the Nation in 1957. It also intended to purchase a Brigade Flag and have it presented to the Nation so that future generations would be aware that a Brigade existed in Scotland.

28. I am grateful to Cathleen Knowles McGuirk for access to the minutes of the Scottish Brigade Old IRA Association, and a copy of the plan of the ambush which was produced as a demonstration aid for the talk on the unsuccessful attempt to rescue Frank Carty from the prison van.

29. I am grateful to Seán Feeney for bringing the newspaper article to my attention.

30. I am grateful to the historian Jim Friel for supplying me with a copy of his article *Mick McLaughlan*. Jim has a personal interest in the prison van story as he has close connections with the Fullerton family from the Garngad. Jim also gave a talk to an audience of the Glasgow Irish on the theme of the Smashing of the Van in the Garngad on 12 May 2007.

31. Cooney, op cit, p.152.

32. Jack House, *The Heart of Glasgow*, Richard Drew Publishing, Glasgow, 1982, p.176.

170

Chapter 9

Conclusion

Any assessment of the rescue attempt would have to concede that it was a failure on several counts. Not only was Frank Carty not freed from the prison van, he also suffered a beating by the police in retaliation for the tragic and unintentional death of their comrade Inspector Johnston. It was officially stated that the 4th May was the first time for many years in which any police official accompanying a prison van had been furnished with firearms. Evidently the police were taking no chances with Brigadier Carty given his two previous jailbreaks and high-ranking position in the IRA. The only other incident involving the wounding of a policeman during this period in Scotland was in October 1920 when an officer stumbled upon an arms raid on a Territorial Army Drill Hall in Bothwell in Lanarkshire. On neither occasion was it planned to open fire on the police.

The anxieties expressed by Liam Mellows, the IRA Quartermaster General, on his visit to Glasgow that an ambush would jeopardise the smuggling of arms and ammunition and lead to a clampdown on the IRA proved prophetic. As the *Daily Record* put it, "It was not until an afternoon in the month of May 1921, that the people of Scotland were brought to realise the immenseness, and the thoroughness of the Irish Republican Movement in Scotland."[1] A notebook found in a Glasgow tenement disclosed a list of firearms and explosives collected from a widespread area and the largest ever IRA arms cache was discovered on the very day of the ambush. Other arrests had been made from time to time, but the repeated injunctions from headquarters for caution in the securing and transport of arms, were for the most part effective in keeping the IRA clear of the authorities. The numerous incidents of drilling filed in police reports, that took place in remote places like the Campsie Hills and Carman Hill, had deflected attention away from the more serious business of swelling the IRA's armoury.

Several high-ranking officers were detained and there was a corresponding reduction in IRA activity in the period that followed the arrests. The success of the police in arresting a significant number of men that were on active service on the 4th May demonstrated that the intelligence forces had a pretty firm idea of the identities of leading IRA personnel in the west of Scotland.

The defence committee was unable to pay all the legal fees for the defence counsel and there were disputes about who should be paying the fees. As late as October 1922, a request was made to the Cabinet of Dáil Éireann to grant £4,000 in order to cover all expenses incurred in Scotland.[2]

The attack on the van was planned without the knowledge of the Army Executive, which, if it had been consulted, would probably have rejected it. The official IRA plan to rescue Carty at sea would seem to have had a better chance of success and Michael O'Carroll felt that, had it gone ahead, the anti IRA outcry that accompanied the trial could have been avoided.

In an atmosphere of urgency, given that Carty was under sentence of death, together with the need for on the spot decisions, individual initiative, organisation and leadership, there may have been an element of confusion. Commandant D.P. Walsh was probably right when he told Charles J. McGuinness that to call off the Glasgow plan, "would shatter the whole Republican movement here". By the time he arrived in Glasgow, the plans were already advanced, and the idea of holding up a prison van and rescuing a high-ranking Republican would have been a far more exciting prospect than the routine drilling and acquisition of arms and munitions that the volunteers were accustomed to.

The IRA volunteers who took part in the rescue bid cannot be blamed for the failure of the Glasgow plan. They showed intelligence, maturity and courage despite their youth. Their community regarded them as heroes, as was shown by the huge 'welcome home' functions organised on their behalf. The fact that the friends and families of the arrested men were willing to perjure themselves in a Scottish court showed they had an immense loyalty to Ireland and her government in her hour of need. The President of the Irish Republic, Éamon de Valera acknowledged this solidarity in 1922 when he stated, "Of all the children of Irish race in foreign lands, none have been more faithful than you in Scotland."[3]

President of the Irish Republic, Éamon de Valera.

Many of the men, who served in the Scottish Brigade and later returned to Ireland, looked back on their time spent on active service in Scotland as glorious days. Michael O'Carroll summed up his opinion of the Glasgow Irish when he said, "The people of Glasgow and the west of Scotland - the first, second and third generations of the Irish - I will always remember them - their loyalty, their sincerity and the ideals which were in their minds. They were wonderful."[4]

Whether or not one agrees with the men of 1916 – and their successors in the War of Independence – no one can deny the courage and determination of these men and women. They were deeply committed to the cause of Irish freedom and many of them suffered greatly for their idealism. After a world war that was supposedly fought for the rights of small nations to self-determination, which was only another word for government by consent, Britain's position in Ireland was politically untenable. The purpose of the War of Independence was to drive that point home beyond recall and it was a war that need never have happened had Britain not been so unwilling to grant Ireland its national rights.

In writing this book I hope I have given some recognition not only to the boys who attempted to smash the van, but also to the thousands of unsung and forgotten men and women of the Scottish Brigade of the Irish Republican Army, Cumann na mBan, Na Fianna Éireann, Sinn Féin and the wider Irish community, who were faithful to Ireland and the Republican ideal during the revolutionary period from 1916 to 1921.

Notes

1. From an article about the rescue bid in the 19 August 1933 edition of the *Daily Record*.
2. Art O'Brien MS.8442, Letters in relation to the Glasgow cases, National Library of Ireland; A13942 S. Dougan Account Mrs Boyle, Glasgow, Military Archives.
3. *Poblacht na hÉireann* (Scottish edition), 18 November 1922.
4. John Cooney, 'The Irish Republican Brotherhood in Scotland: The Untold Stories of Andrew Fagan and Michael O'Carroll', *Celebrating Columba: Irish Scottish Connections 597-1997*, TM Devine and JF McMillan (eds), (John Donald, Edinburgh, 1999), p.152.

Appendix 1: Scottish Brigade of the Irish Republican Army, 1921

BATTALION	DISTRICTS	PARADE HALLS
FIRST		
A Company	Glasgow – based in Maryhill	Banba Halls 1919-1923
B Company	Glasgow – based in Bridgeton	Castle Street, Merkland Street, Partick and Muslin Street, Bridgeton
C Company	Govan and Kinning Park	Boilermakers Hall, Govan
D Company	Baillieston, Shettleston, Tollcross and Parkhead	
E Company	Uddingston and Mossend	
F Company	Clydebank, Dalmuir, Paisley, Duntocher and Barrhead	
G Company	Glasgow Central	171 Renfield Street and later Terence MacSwiney Hall, Trongate
H Company	Cambuslang, Wellshot, Carmyle and Rutherglen	
I Company	Dumbarton, Renton, Alexandria, Cardross and Kirkintilloch	
SECOND		
A Company	Motherwell and Craigneuk	
B Company	Wishaw and Newmains	
C Company	Blantyre and Bothwell	
D Company	Coatbridge, Coatdyke, Airdrie, Whifflet and Calderbank	Shamrock Hall
E Company	Hamilton, Burnbank, Cadzow and Larkhall	

BATTALION	DISTRICTS	PARADE HALLS
SECOND		
F Company	Bellshill, Mossend, Holytown and New Stevenston	McCann Hall
G Company	Cadzow	
H Company	Cleland and Carfin	
THIRD		
A Company	Edinburgh, Leith and Portobello	
B Company	Broxburn, Bathgate, Winchurgh, Philipstown, Niddrie, Shotts, Uphall and Linlithgow	
C Company	Mid and West Calder, Addiewell and Stoneyburn	
D Company	Falkirk	
E Company	Bannockburn, Denny, Bonnybridge, Cowie and Stirlingshire	
FOURTH		
D Company	Dundee and district	
Not allotted (3rd and 4th Battalion)	Buckhaven, Methilhill, Lochgelly, Cowdenbeath, Lochore, Kinross–shire	
FIFTH		
B Company	Greenock, Gourock and Port Glasgow	St Mary's Hall and Duncan Street Hall

Appendix 2: The Smashing of the Van
(Street ballad of the Glasgow Irish written by Mick McLaughlan)

'Twas on the fourth of May, boys,
In nineteen twenty one,
That the news ran through all Scotland
That a daring deed was done,
Done by a band of heroes
To release an Irishman,
They assembled in the High Street
And they smashed the prison van.

Chorus:

Here's to the boys who done it!
Their hearts were staunch and true,
Every man who played his part that day
Was Irish through and through.
Side by side they stood there,
Revolvers in their hands,
Did that gallant band of rebels
When they smashed the prison van.

Our clever Glasgow Polis
Were soon upon the scene.
They arrested every Irishman
Connected with Sinn Féin.
They arrested Father MacRory
An R.C. clergyman,
Which only showed their ignorance
At the Smashing of the Van.

When the fight was over
The boys they did retreat.
Stirton said, "Down Rottenrow"
Macdonald said, "Down High Street"
Ross said, "Down the Drygate,
That was the way they ran."
But they only proved three liars
At the Smashing of the Van.

Now the trial is over,
The Crown case it did fail,
Though Stirton did his level best
To put them all in jail.
Defended by those counsellors,
Mackay and Sandeman
Sure, the jury said "Not Guilty"
To the smashers of the van.

Appendix 3: Daily Duties in Duke Street Prison

(Written by Éamonn Mooney in Duke Street Prison while awaiting trial on a charge of murder in connection with the prison van episode)

When we get out of Duke Street, no more porridge for our tea
When we get out of prison O how happy we shall be
No more drinking pints of water and no more marching round the ring
When we get out of Duke Street we will dance and we will sing.

No more folding of your blankets, no more walking 'cross the floor
No more handing out your skilly pot, to the warder at the door
No more asking for requests, and no more scrubbing out your cell
When we get out of Duke Street we will fairly kick up hell.

No more screwing up your faces, when the warder's back is turned
(aside) "what are ye in for?"
No more supping for your breakfast of the milk that hath been churned
No more gazing out the window and no more thinking of your fate
When we get out of Duke Street, we won't linger round the gate.

No more reading regulations, no more scribbling on the wall
No more rising up so early, O no more of that at all
No more listening on a Sunday to the "Bible Thumpers" psalm
When we get out of Duke Street, O we will not care a damn!

No more standing to attention when the Governor visits you
No more marking of your work sheet by the prison labour "Buroo"
For there's a good day coming for the fighters of Sinn Féin
When we get out of Duke Street, we will smile when they remain.

When we get out of prison we will shout and we shall sing
That we do not give a rifle shot for his Majesty the King
For we are the jolly good Sinn Féiners a brave and gallant little band
And when we get out of Duke Street we shall fight for Ireland.

And now that we are out of Duke Street and once more again are free
We'll go down, to the Major John McBride Club, where a concert there will be
Éamonn Mooney will sing "Right you Are" as he did in days of yore
Then we'll finish up the evening with a grand old Ceilidhe Mor.

Danny Boy – No 5 Cell 1ˢᵗ Flat. Duke Street Prison, July 1921

Bibliography

1. Public Records

National Archives of Scotland: HH055/00062, HH055/00063, HH055/00065, HH055/00066, HH055/00067, HH055/00068, HH055/00069, HH055/00070, HH055/00071, 'Irish Disturbances'.
Public Records Office, Kew, London: 'Report on the Activities of Revolutionary Organisations in the United Kingdom', CP3055 1 June 1921; CP 3074 23 June 1921, Cab 24/125.
Bureau of Military History: statement by witness, Joseph Booker, NAI, BMH papers, WS 776; statement by witness, Patrick Mills, NAI, BMH papers, WS 777 statement by witness, James Byrne, NAI, BMH papers, WS 828.
National Library of Ireland: Art O'Brien MS.8442, Letters in relation to the Glasgow cases; A13942 S. Dougan Account Mrs Boyle, Glasgow Sligo County Library. Statement of Military Activities of Frank Carty, late O.C. 4th Brigade, 3rd Western Division, 1935.

2. Other unpublished material

The Éamonn Mooney Papers are in the possession of Cathleen Knowles McGuirk.

3. Periodicals, journals, and newspapers consulted

An tÓglach, The Bulletin, Daily Record, The Evening Citizen, The Evening Standard, The Evening Times, Forward, The Glasgow Herald, Glasgow Observer, Irish Post, Irish Press, The Irish Times, Poblacht na hÉireann (Scottish edition), *Radical Scotland, The Roscommon Herald, The Scotsman, Scottish Catholic Observer, Scots Law Times, The Times, The Ulster Herald, The Western People.*

4. Books, articles pamphlets and university theses consulted and used

Blake, Frances M., *The Irish Civil War 1922-1923*, Information on Ireland, London, 1986.
Broom, John, *John MacLean*, MacDonald Publishers, Loanhead, 1973.

Burrowes, John, 'The Glasgow Outrage', *Great Glasgow Stories*, (Mainstream Publishing, Edinburgh, 1998.

Burrowes, John, *Irish: The Remarkable Saga of a Nation and a City*, Mainstream Publishing, Edinburgh, 2003.

Canning, Rev. Bernard J., *Irish-Born Secular Priests in Scotland, 1829-1979*, Bookmag, Inverness, 1979.

Cavanagh, Colm M., *Derry Jail*, Guildhall Press, Derry, 1990.

Cooney, John, 'The Irish Republican Brotherhood in Scotland: The Untold Stories of Andrew Fagan and Michael O'Carroll', *Celebrating Columba: Irish Scottish Connections 597-1997*, TM Devine and JF McMillan (eds.), John Donald, Edinburgh, 1999.

Coyle, Stephen, 'A Scottish Gael Who Died for the Irish Republic', *Ballingeary Historical Society Journal*, 2006.

Coyle, Stephen, 'William Gillies - Portrait of a Patriot', *Scottish Workers Republic*, Spring 1997.

Dalton, Des, *Sinn Féin: 100 Years of Revolution 1905-2005,* Irish Freedom Press, Dublin 2005.

Farry, Michael, *Sligo 1914-1921: A Chronicle of Conflict*, Killoran Press, Trim, County Meath, 1992.

Farry, Michael, *The Aftermath of Revolution: Sligo 1921-23*, University College of Dublin Press, 2000.

Finlay, Richard, *Independent and Free*, John Donald Publishers, Edinburgh, 1994.

Foreman, Carol, 'Police Inspector Shot Dead in High Street', *Glasgow Curiosities,* John Donald Publishers Ltd, Edinburgh, 1998.

Gallagher, Tom, *Glasgow the Uneasy Peace*, Manchester University Press, 1987.

Grant, Douglas, *The Thin Blue Line*: *The Story of the Glasgow Police*, John Long, London, 1973.

Greaves, Desmond, *Liam Mellows and the Irish Revolution*, Lawrence & Wishart, London, 1971.

Handley, James, *The Irish in Modern Scotland*, Cork University Press, 1947.

Hart, Peter, 'Operations Abroad: The IRA in Britain, 1919-23', *The English Historical Review*, Volume 115, No 460, February 2000.

Hopkinson, Michael, *The Irish War of Independence*, Gill & McMillan, Dublin, 2004.

House, Jack, *The Heart of Glasgow*, Richard Drew Publishing, Glasgow, 1982.

Jackson, T.A., *Ireland Her Own*, Lawrence & Wishart, London, 1976.

Kelly, Billy, *Sworn to Be Free: The Complete Book of IRA Jailbreaks 1918-1921*, (O'Donoghue, Florence (ed.), Anvil Books, Tralee, 1971.

King, Elspeth, *The Strike of the Calton Weavers 1787*, Glasgow Museums and Art Galleries, 1987.

McGuffin, John, Mulheron, Joseph, *Charles 'Nomad' McGuinness*, Irish Resistance Books, Derry, 2002.

McDougall, I. (ed), *Militant Miners*, Polygon Books, Edinburgh, 1981.

McGuinness, Charles John, *Nomad*, Methuen, London, 1934.

Mac Eoin, Uinseann, *Survivors*, Argenta, Dublin, 1987.

Maguire, Michael, 'From Across the Irish Sea: The Irish in Britain and the Making of 1916', *1916 - We Remember*, Cumann na Poblachta, London, 1991.

Milton, Nan, *John MacLean: In the Rapids of Revolution*, Allison & Busby Ltd, London, 1978.

Neeson, Eoin, *The Civil War 1922-23*, Poolbeg Press, Swords, 1989.

Murphy, Brian S., 'The Stone of Destiny: Father John Fahy (1894-1969), Lia Fail and Smallholder Radicalism in Modern Irish Society' in *Radical Irish Priests 1660–1970*, (ed. Gerard Moran), Four Courts Press Ltd, Dublin, 1998.

Noyles, Alfred, *The Accusing Ghost or Justice for Casement*, Victor Gollancz Ltd, London.

Ó Baoighill, Pádraig, *Óglach na Rossan*, Dublin, 1994.

Ó Brádaigh, Ruairi, *Dilseacht: The Story of Comdt. General Tom Maguire and the Second (All-Ireland) Dáil*, Elo Press Ltd, Dublin, 1997.

Ó Catháin, Máirtín, *Irish Republicanism in Scotland 1858-1916: Fenians in Exile*, Irish Academic Press, Dublin, 2007.

Ó Catháin, Máirtín, 'A Winnowing Spirit: Sinn Féin in Scotland, 1905-1938', *New Perspectives on The Irish in Scotland*, (ed. Martin J. Mitchell) John Donald, Edinburgh, 2008.

Ó Catháin, Máirtín, *Michael Collins and Scotland*. Forthcoming 2009.

O'Donnell, Ruan (Ed.), *The Impact of the 1916 Rising*, Irish Academic Press, Dublin, 2008.

O'Donovan, Donal, *Kevin Barry and His Time*, Glendale Press, County Dublin, 1989.

O'Hagan, Andrew, *The Missing*, Picador, 1995.

Patterson, Iain D, 'The Activities of Irish Republican Physical Force Organisations in Scotland 1919-21', *Scottish Historical Review*, Volume LXXII I No 193, April 1995.

Potter, David W., *The Life and Times of Patsy Gallagher*, Parrs Ward Press, Manchester, 2000.

Ritchie, David, *Sinn Fein and the Scottish Office 1919-1923*, PhD thesis, Edinburgh University, 2008.

Rose, Paul, *The Manchester Martyrs: A Fenian Tragedy,* Lawrence & Wishart, 1970.

Skelton, Douglas, 'Ambush', *Blood On the Thistle*, Mainstream Publishing, Glasgow, 1992.

Stewart, Bob, *Breaking the Fetters*, Lawrence & Wishart, London, 1967.

Tuckett, Angela, *The Scottish Trade Union Congress: The First 80 Years 1897-1977*, Mainstream Publishers, Edinburgh, 1986.

Twohig, Patrick J, *Green Tears for Hecuba: Ireland's fight For Freedom*, Tower Books, County Cork, 1984.

Wood, Ian, *John Wheatley*, Manchester University Press, 1990.

Younger, Calton, *Ireland's Civil War*, Fontana, Glasgow, 1982.

Index

185

186